Lincoln's Burial Grounds: Commemorating the city's dead

Editor: ANDREW WALKER

Published by
The Survey of Lincoln, 2023

ISBN 978-0-9931263-8-3

ACKNOWLEDGEMENTS

Thanks to all of the contributors to this collection for their enthusiasm for the project. I would like to express my gratitude to John Herridge, Michael J. Jones and Geoff Tann for their help with proof reading and helping to prepare the text for publication. The assistance of staff at Lincoln Central Library and Lincolnshire Archives is gratefully acknowledged, as is the prompt assistance of employees from a number of photographic archives.

The Survey of Lincoln wishes to extend its thanks to the John Dawber Trust for its generous financial support with the production of this volume, and also to the Lincolnshire Co-op.

Andrew Walker

Dedication
This work is dedicated to the memory of Beryl George, a much-missed committee member of The Survey of Lincoln and a regular contributor to previous volumes in this book series.

Introduction

Andrew Walker

This edited collection in The Survey of Lincoln's thematic series examines the city's treatment of its dead over time. Although initially there was some scepticism among members about this as a book theme, it quickly became apparent that there was much of interest to be researched and written on the subject.

The work explores the burial of the dead within the city, the sites where this has taken place over two millennia, and the ways in which the city's deceased have been remembered. Whilst the focus is principally upon examining the buildings and structures associated with the dead and their commemoration, attention is also paid in the more recent past to those engaged in individuals' after-life care, including the city's memorial masons, undertakers and funeral carriage suppliers. Several chapters also examine the changing customs and practices associated with funerals.

The gravestone of William McBeath in Canwick Road Old Cemetery. McBeath was co-founder of Rangers Football Club. (*Michael J. Jones*).

Chapters by Michael J. Jones, Alastair MacIntosh and Geoff Tann explore the evidence relating to the dead during Roman times. As is discussed, in the early Roman era it seemed that cremation was favoured over the burial of bodies – inhumation – which became more common from the mid-third century onwards. It is estimated that between about 50,000 to 100,000 individuals were buried in some form during the Roman era outside the walls of the city. The principal archaeological finds relating to the dead of the Roman period since the eighteenth century are examined by Michael J. Jones, and Alastair MacIntosh's chapter reports on the most recent discoveries. In both chapters, improvements in scientific analysis are discussed which have yielded much more information about the dead than had been possible previously. Geoff Tann's chapter shows how burials also took place at individual villas outside Lincoln. It is clear that there are many more sites of Roman cremation and inhumation to be discovered within the city and its immediate surroundings.

Burials and cemeteries within the medieval period are explored, from the Anglo-Scandinavian in Michael J. Jones's chapter to graves at long-since abandoned burial sites, such as St Katherine's Priory, examined by Colin Brown, and the churchyard of the parish of St Clement, considered by Naomi Field. Chris Johnson provides some thoughts on where the burial ground of the medieval Jewish community might be located. During the medieval period, 47 parish churches are known to have stood in Lincoln, many with their own churchyards. Rob Wheeler's chapter details the ways in which some of these grounds continued

The war grave of 18-year-old Aircraftwoman Daphne Norman, Newport Cemetery. (*Andrew Walker*).

to have a life beyond that of their associated church, looking particularly at examples such as the churchyards of St Mary Crackpole and St Cuthbert.

Other specific burial grounds are considered prior to the major reform of such spaces in the mid-nineteenth century. Erin Bell's chapter examines the burial ground of the Religious Society of Friends (Quakers), opened in the later seventeenth century. Although no longer visible, this was situated between Beaumont Fee and Park Street. The Friends' Meeting House of 1689 is located within the burial ground. Lesley Church's chapter on St Paul-in-the-Bail considers the long history of this churchyard, now closed, but still a much-used public space next to the junction of Bailgate and Westgate.

Lesley's chapter notes the challenges faced when St Paul-in-the-Bail's churchyard became full. This was a common and much-reported problem within Lincoln's city centre by the mid-nineteenth century. Closures of Lincoln's churchyards, stopping further burials, were ordered following an official visit from a member of the Central Board of Health in 1854. An Order in Council prohibited burials after 1 November 1855 in almost all the existing burial grounds. The results of this prohibition included the formation of several burial boards within the city which led to new cemeteries being opened, including those at Eastgate, Canwick Road, and St Swithin's new cemetery on Washingborough Road. Many of these new burial sites were on the edge of the city, returning to the preferred practice

Rebecca and William Smalley are remembered on this ornate headstone, one of many highly decorative graves in St Peter-in-Eastgate Cemetery, Langworthgate. (*Andrew Walker*).

of the Romans. The development and construction of these new sites of burial was not always straightforward, as is made clear in chapters by Arthur Ward and myself, which build upon earlier work on the Canwick Road cemeteries by Derek Broughton in The Survey of Lincoln's earlier volume, *South-East Lincoln*. It is sad to see the current poor state of repair of the chapels designed by Michael Drury as part of the Canwick Road cemetery development.

At various times in the city's history, specific burial grounds have been in use for somewhat marginalised groups within society. Nigel Horner's chapter examines some of the city's welfare institutions, such as the workhouse and The Lawn Hospital and the places of rest in which their inhabitants were sometimes placed.

Several chapters examine remembrance of the city's war dead. Paul Hickman's chapter draws attention to a number of graves and memorials within the current boundaries of the city that are associated with nineteenth-century campaign veterans. Andrew Priestley's chapter looks at some of the war graves in Eastgate Cemetery, and suggests that there are rather more present than are listed by the Commonwealth War Graves Commission. My chapter on Newport Cemetery examines how the war dead have been remembered here, and notes how there are now considerably fewer war graves on this site than there were immediately after the Second World War. Two chapters in the volume by Arthur Ward and myself detail some of the world war-related memorials in the city, including those in workplaces and other sites, as well as the well-known memorials in public spaces across the city. A compendium of such memorials would be a useful additional project. Hazel Kent's chapter examines the ways in which the city's civilian war dead in the Second World War were commemorated. In Derwin Gregory's chapter, attention is paid to how a well-known local landmark on the edge of the city was prepared for use as an emergency Second World War mortuary.

How individual lives have been commemorated immediately after their passing is considered in the volume. Chapters by Lesley Church and Ken Redmore look at some prominent nineteenth-century citizens and how their funerals were conducted and their lives marked in the surviving memorial stones. With the use of some company records, Georgina Collingwood investigates the important role of memorial masons in producing the headstones and other commemorative structures within the city's cemeteries. The later restoration of such memorials is considered by Gary Rook, who played a key part in arranging the recent restoration of the grave of a prominent Lincoln industrialist.

The task of getting the bodies to their final resting places is explored in contributions by Geoff Tann, who examines one Lincoln-based funeral carriage supplier, and Adam

Cartwright, whose chapter sheds light on the work of some nineteenth- and twentieth-century undertakers.

Consideration of the dead in the city's more recent past, and in particular, changing burial practice, is the focus of a chapter by an experienced funeral director, Jonathan Whiting. The relatively late arrival of a crematorium is also considered, as is, in Abigail Hunt's chapter, the opening of Lincoln's most recent burial ground, Long Leys Cemetery.

From these varied chapters, it becomes clear that, by examining the treatment of the city's dead and the changes in this practice over time, much can also be learned about the economic, social, cultural and spiritual values of the living. Metaphorically, there is still much more to be unearthed.

Canwick Road New Cemetery lodge and entrance, Washingborough Road. (*Andrew Walker*).

Archaeology and Lincoln's Early Cemeteries

Michael J. Jones

For several hundred years during the Roman period (c.AD50-c.400) in Lincoln, and for a greater length of time from the Anglo-Scandinavian period beginning in c.AD900, cemeteries formed a large constituent of the space taken up by the urban settlement. By law, burial in the Roman world was only allowed outside the town boundary. There were variations to that rule, linked to the rise of Christianity, from the fifth century, but the surviving settlement was for several centuries not a large one. By 900, and the urban revival, burial in the growing town was largely confined to churchyards. In terms of numbers, it can be estimated that between 50,000 and 100,000 individuals were interred in Lincoln during the Roman era, initially in cremations, but during the third century increasingly as inhumations. A greater number of inhumations must have occurred during the long medieval era, linked to at least 46 parish churches, the cathedral, and several friaries and monastic establishments. Sadly, it is only in recent decades that we have been able to achieve some scientific analysis of the remains, an area in which there have been notable advances.

Roman Lincoln, cAD50–cAD400

It was in the larger towns of Roman Britain, and particularly in the later Roman period, that graves were laid out most formally. The presence of many Roman burials, or at least the finds associated with them such as cremation vessels or tombstones, was noted from the late seventeenth and eighteenth centuries: the modern town was expanding over the suburban areas formerly marked by Roman cemeteries. This trend continued into the nineteenth century as the increase in industrialisation gathered pace. One particular concentration was in the area of Monson Street, off lower High Street, marking where the cremated remains of several legionaries must have been

The tombstone of Caius Valerius, standard-bearer of the Ninth Legion, found on the South Common. (*Reproduced with the kind permission of Lincoln Museum*).

The tombstone of Flavius Helius Grecus, a Greek in Roman Lincoln. (*Reproduced with the kind permission of Lincoln Museum*).

placed. Other tombstones were among the re-used sculptural material incorporated in certain locations into the fourth-century re-build of the city wall. One documents a dedication to his wife by a town councillor (*decurio*), Aurelius Senecio – for years an exhibit in the British Museum's Roman Britain gallery. Various inscriptions demonstrate the cosmopolitan nature of the population, with Gauls and Greeks among those documented. Discoveries of burials and cremation pots are still being made. Even fringe areas to the rear of the traders' houses that lined the street frontages and backing towards the watercourses could be used for burial (see Alastair MacIntosh's later chapter). As these recent discoveries suggest, there were greater variations in burial types than was previously acknowledged. Bodies were normally dressed in clothing, but very rarely do textiles survive. From discoveries in the last decade, we now know that the cemeteries extended northwards as far as Riseholme Road and southwards to South Common and St Catherine's. Other burials beyond this boundary can sometimes be linked to individual villa establishments in the countryside immediately outside the town. (See Geoff Tann's chapter.) More remains of the presumed villa were discovered by Allen Archaeology, ironically in advance of the creation of the Long Leys Road cemetery.

Sub-Roman – Early Medieval Lincoln, cAD400–cAD900

There was a significant change in practice following the demise of the Roman city and the loss of the vast majority of the population. Two particular excavation sites that contained burials constitute a significant proportion of the scarce evidence for the nature of Lincoln in these poorly-documented centuries. The site of the former Roman city appears to have continued for a century or more as a British stronghold. Part of the evidence for this hypothesis is the fact that there were no large-scale Anglo-Saxon cemeteries within 25km of Lincoln. During this time its centre of power may have remained at the location of the forum. Within the forum courtyard, what would become St Paul-in-the Bail originated as a timber church, probably erected before AD600. The sequence of burials around it began no later than the seventh and eighth centuries, and included a special one at the centre of a chapel succeeding the early church. The body here had been removed, but the stone-lined grave still contained an exotic bronze hanging-bowl. A few other burials of this period were found towards the southern edge of the lower city, to the south-east of St Peter-at-Arches

Detail of the tombstone of a Roman woman, Claudia Crysis, who lived until the age of 90. (*Reproduced with the kind permission of Lincoln Museum*).

church – another structure probably re-using elements of surviving Roman public buildings and an early Christian focus. Most of the burials here were of women: the significance of this fact is uncertain. One has been the subject of a facial reconstruction currently on display in Lincoln Museum.

Anglo-Scandinavian and medieval Lincoln, cAD900-cAD1500

By the later tenth century, these two early Christian cemeteries belonged to parish churches and were being joined by many more as Lincoln again expanded rapidly to become a vibrant Anglo-Scandinavian town. At least 32 of them were in place before c.1100. Such a proliferation is a phenomenon confined to larger towns in the east of England, where many were founded by the lesser aristocracy. In due course, they numbered about 46, each with its own graveyard. David Stocker has analysed their possible origins and locations – a complex pattern. Many occupied corner plots, some being 'gate-guardians', others adjoining markets (of various shapes and sizes), and others merely rectilinear strip plots on the street frontage. Quite a number were planted within urban estates. The Bail was apparently a prestigious 'reserved' area in the immediate pre-Conquest period, with the four quarters each having a parish church associated with the four principal lords owning property in the city (including St Clement: see Naomi Field's chapter). There were further cemeteries associated with the cathedral – including that belonging to the minster predating the Norman foundation – and with the monastic establishments. Chris Johnson writes below regarding the possible location of the medieval Jewish cemetery.

Large areas of two parish graveyards, those of St Mark and St Paul-in-the-Bail, have been extensively excavated, but, sadly, before reliable analysis of the human remains could be achieved. Several hundred graves were encountered at each, earlier burials often being disturbed by later grave-cuts. The St Mark site produced an impressive collection of pre-Conquest monuments, mainly decorated grave-covers but also including some headstones and footstones. This assemblage suggests a link to local merchants and a collaborative foundation – probably in common with nearby St Mary-le-Wigford. Elements of several other graveyards have been excavated in different parts of the city in connection with urban redevelopment. This sample has allowed some anatomical and pathological analysis to be undertaken, enabling us, for instance, to compare the stature, longevity and health of the populations of different parts of the city and those associated with friary sites.

Scientific techniques are improving constantly, as a most recently-investigated example demonstrates: the discovery of part of an early church or chapel inside the east gate of Lincoln Castle also included several graves. In particular, the application of stable isotope and DNA analysis provides clues to the origins of the individuals found there. It is notable that several of those excavated had grown up far from Lincoln, some even abroad. Most died during the eleventh century, and none lived beyond the age of about 45.

With the decline in the city's fortunes from the late thirteenth century, certain parishes became depopulated, as a survey of 1428 clearly indicates. Some were united with other parishes and their graveyards were abandoned. This trend continued until it was formally rationalised by the formal Act of Union of Parishes in 1549. (See Rob Wheeler's chapter, below). As another article by David Stocker demonstrated, the friaries might initially have benefited from the availability of redundant church fabric before they too were closed in the 1530s. Some of the parish churchyards were left as open spaces, and many can still be discerned on Padley's 1842 map. Yet, as their ground-levels had been raised by the displacement effect of so many interments, they were in due course prone to later disturbance from new developments and road-building as the modern city grew again. The former church site of St Nicholas, at the junction of Newport and Church Lane, is just one that makes this point clearly, as it still largely preserved at its medieval level, considerably higher than that of the present street.

Skull and reconstruction of the face of a mid-Saxon woman found in Silver Street excavations, 1973–4. (*Reproduced with the kind permission of Lincoln Museum*).

Some other finds, Roman to post-Medieval

Several other archaeological investigations have revealed human remains, of different periods and in different contexts. They range from mysterious to possibly criminal activity – such as a young Roman woman buried in a shallow grave by the waterside, a male burial between the road surfaces inside the Castle's West Gate, and a grave within the garden of a property known to have belonged to a Quaker. Near to the second of these, and of much later date, some graves were encountered during service-trenching adjacent to the Crown Court, probably those of debtors who had been imprisoned. Felons and those executed were buried in separate areas. At a later date, the graves of criminals were dug within the Lucy Tower.

Archaeology has much more to tell us about this important aspect of the city's long past.

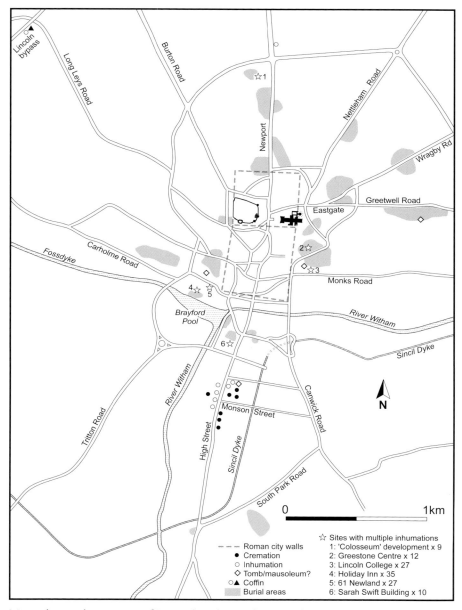

Map indicating known areas of Roman burial grounds. Drawn by Dave Watt.

Legend:

- - - Roman city walls
● Cremation
○ Inhumation
◇ Tomb/mausoleum?
○▲ Coffin
▨ Burial areas

☆ Sites with multiple inhumations
1: 'Colosseum' development x 9
2: Greestone Centre x 12
3: Lincoln College x 27
4: Holiday Inn x 35
5: 61 Newland x 27
6: Sarah Swift Building x 10

RECENT DISCOVERIES OF ROMAN INHUMATION CEMETERIES IN LINCOLN

Alastair MacIntosh

Unlike other comparable Roman cities, such as Gloucester, Winchester and London, no single large cemetery has yet been excavated from Lincoln, and the total number of burials recovered up to the present day represents only a small fraction of the overall number of burials. Many of the early finds of funerary remains show a strong bias towards either cremation burials or monumental tombstones, and it is possible that plainer inhumation burials, with few or no accompanying grave goods, were lost without being recorded in any way, perhaps even without being recognised as Roman.

Although cremation burials and their associated goods are in themselves useful and informative, there are many physical characteristics and attributes of the dead that cannot be measured or identified in cremated remains. For example, it is mainly through detailed analysis of intact skeletal remains that archaeologists can identify the age and sex of the deceased, and observe the physical marks of disease and injury. It is therefore of great importance that when inhumation burials are located during building projects a full archaeological investigation can be undertaken.

Over the last ten years a handful of large and fortuitously located development projects have between them revealed around 120 articulated Roman inhumation burials in four discrete areas, namely Newland, Newport, the High Street, and the eastern hillside. These sites were all identified during the planning process, and works were conducted by local professional archaeological companies under an agreed scheme of investigation which was paid for by the relevant developer.

Newland

Sixty-two inhumation burials from the Newland cemetery have been found over two individual digs undertaken prior to the construction of a student accommodation block in 2015 and the extension to a hotel in 2016. The burials comprised 23 likely/possible males, 17 likely/possible females, nine children, and 13 whose age and sex could not be determined. The burials were in varying states of preservation and for the most part were poorly furnished with grave goods. No monuments were recovered from either site. Detailed analysis of the bones showed that several individuals had suffered in life from the physical impacts of hard manual work, resulting in damage to joints and vertebrae. Although some had clearly been buried in coffins, indicated by soil staining, small remnants of preserved wood and the presence of coffin nails around the grave cut, some had apparently been buried without them. This can be inferred from the ease with which later burials had cut through earlier ones, in some cases removing the feet or the head. Taken together, these factors suggest that the Newland cemetery was populated by those of a relatively low social status. The wider cemetery of which these two sites form a part appears to have been in use throughout the Roman period, dating from the first century AD. The later excavation also found a large late Roman ditch to the south of the site which has been tentatively interpreted as the southern boundary marker for the cemetery area. Both of these excavations were undertaken by PCAS Archaeology Ltd.

Brayford Wharf East

Ten inhumation burials and one cremation were identified during excavation of drainage facilities for a new university building, between Brayford Wharf East and the High Street, south of the railway line. The discovery was unexpected as previous evaluation of the site had revealed no evidence of human remains. All but one of the inhumations were children, and most were of newborns. One of these burials was deliberately covered by an intact Roman roof tile, known as a *tegula*. No grave goods could confidently be ascribed to the inhumation

burials, as the ground in which they were dug was made up of earlier Roman dumped deposits themselves containing many sherds of pottery. The cremation burial was contained within a grey ware jar and has been dated to the late Roman period, possibly the fourth century AD. This and the following sites were excavated by Allen Archaeology Ltd.

Newport

In 2014 works undertaken ahead of the construction of 'The Colosseum' residential development along Newport revealed nine burials. Several of the graves contained hobnails, indicating that the bodies were buried wearing

Roman roof tile (*tegula*) used to cover an infant burial on the site of the University of Lincoln Sarah Swift building. (*Alastair MacIntosh*).

Roman structure discovered to the west of Newport, identified as a probable roadside mausoleum. (*Photograph courtesy of Allen Archaeology Ltd*).

boots, and presumably therefore were also fully clothed. This is supported by the find of a bracelet still on the wrist of one of the inhumation burials. Perhaps the most exciting discovery was a possible stone mausoleum, found in association with disarticulated human remains, coins and Roman pottery. The structure was built on to the bedrock with multiple courses of dry stone construction surviving on three of its four sides. While it is not possible to say for certain that the structure was a tomb, its size and location make such an interpretation plausible, and if correct this would be the first example of such a structure to be found in Lincoln.

The Eastern Hillside

Two separate excavations to the east of the Roman city have revealed a previously unidentified burial area on the hillside. In 2012 groundworks at Lincoln College produced 25 articulated Roman skeletons. They ranged in age from around 4–5 years old to 60, although most were older than 45, and of the burials whose sex could be determined, 13 were male and seven

Late fourth-century 'crossbow' fibula recovered from a grave on the site of the Lincoln College Greestone Centre building. (*Photograph courtesy of Allen Archaeology Ltd*).

were female. The population was in generally good health, with little evidence of joint disease or spinal injuries. The excavation also found evidence of a previously unknown Roman road forming a southern boundary to the burial area.

In 2014 an excavation at the site of the new Lincoln UTC at Greestone Place, somewhat further to the north, allowed the recovery of five more individual inhumations, with evidence of several more in the form of disarticulated remains. Two of the inhumations, separated by around 50 years, appear to be of senior officials, as evidenced by the 'crossbow' brooches that each of them wore.

The two sites, though separated by a distance of roughly 200m seem likely to be part of the same wider burial area. This is supported by evidence from a smaller excavation at the outdoor fitness park just south of Lindum Road and roughly equidistant between the two main excavations where a collection of disturbed and disarticulated human remains was found in association with Roman pottery.

Discussion

While keeping in mind the limited sample size, it is possible to make some observations about the people of Roman Lincoln as revealed by these excavations. There is a notable imbalance between male and female burial numbers, with the former outnumbering the latter approximately two to one among those remains that were able to be sexed. The fact that this imbalance persists across all the sites described above implies that it is reflective of the wider burial population, so it seems likely that some process was in action that prevented female children in particular from surviving into adulthood. One possible explanation for this is that the population of Roman Lincoln practised sex-selective infanticide owing to the greater perceived burden presented by female children to their families in Roman culture.

So-called 'deviant' burials make up a relatively large proportion of the total, with several examples of prone and decapitation burials. The most common burial position in Roman contexts is for the body to be laid out lying supine (on its back), and it is possible that differences in burial position reflect cultural or societal differences that existed in life, or perhaps in the circumstances of death. This may be a question that lies beyond the capacity of archaeological investigation to answer fully, but a detailed analysis of burials from across the East Midlands region may at least help to establish the extent and significance of these practices.

No excavation in Lincoln has yet yielded the large numbers of Roman burials that should be expected from a city of this size. It is possible that the growth of the city in the eighteenth and nineteenth centuries has caused wholesale loss of evidence, but if that is the case then it seems strange that it was not remarked upon at the time. The total burial population of Roman Lincoln from its foundation to the end of the Roman period is likely to have been over 100,000 individuals.

When we consider that fewer than 300 intact inhumation and cremation burials have been recorded to date we must accept that any broad inferences drawn from this small sample may be misleading or even wholly incorrect. Furthermore, the burials recovered are not a truly random sample of the total population, but rather comprise a series of different sized windows into it, and so any statistical analysis of attributes such as sex, age, and health may be superseded and even contradicted by later work on any larger groups of burials that may be discovered in the future.

It is highly likely that most of Lincoln's Roman burials remain to be discovered, and thanks to the work of antiquarians and archaeologists over many years it is possible to identify broad areas of the city where such finds are likely to be revealed. Now that the available material includes a greater proportion of intact skeletal remains, archaeologists will be able to look again at their research questions for the city and the wider region, and improve them in light of these new discoveries.

A Rare Roman Timber Coffin Found Beside Long Leys Road

Geoff Tann

Wooden coffins were common in Britain during the Roman period but their survival is exceptionally unusual. Archaeologists commonly find graves with the skeleton and slight soil markings around it where the wooden boards have rotted and been replaced with soil. Frequently, nails are present that fixed the boards together, but many were probably constructed with joints alone. An intact example from about AD120 was found in London in 2005 and described as the only example of its kind found in Britain.

In 1984, substantial pieces of wooden boards from the sides and base of a Roman coffin were discovered during contractors' excavations for foundations of the bypass bridge over Long Leys Road. In that instance, almost all trace of the human skeleton had dissolved and the coffin had filled with soil.

The discovery was unexpected. The author had arranged with the North Lincolnshire Archaeological Unit and the bypass engineers to undertake unpaid archaeological monitoring of the topsoil removal along the bypass route in case archaeological remains were revealed. Several find spots had been made earlier in the project but the topsoil strip between the foot of the steep Burton hillside and the A57 uncovered only relatively recent fragments of tobacco pipes and china. Two or three weeks after that topsoil strip, the author heard anecdotally of Roman metal objects being found on that stretch by metal detector users, but nothing had been officially reported. Puzzled, the author made yet another visit, to find that shallow excavations for road re-alignment at the site of the new bridge had uncovered well-constructed stone foundations, probably for two Roman buildings. Associated pottery indicated a third-century AD date. The Roman remains had been entirely buried by hill-wash from the slope.

The foundations were surveyed and recorded by the author and Mick Clark working late into a Sunday evening. The bypass contractors were also working close by (hence the need for haste) and on one brief visit to watch their excavations, fragments of a wooden plank were machined out of a hole. At that stage it was unclear what had been discovered, but the contractors and road engineers agreed to a brief suspension of that excavation.

The following morning, rapid trowelling established that more extensive remains were still in the ground. It was suspected that two wooden coffins had been destroyed by the machining but one remained substantially intact. Working to a deadline of about five hours, archaeologists recorded what was visible and arranged for the surviving coffin, which

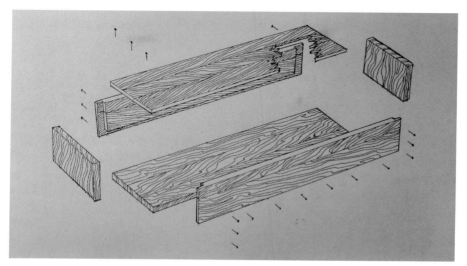

The Roman timber coffin found beside Long Leys Road: exploded diagram (not to scale) by M.V. Clark. *(Reproduced with permission.)*

was preserved in waterlogged conditions, to be removed. It was lifted out by machine and transported (requiring seven people) off-site for closer examination in a less stressful environment. Salvage recording of the discovery severely restricted the information that it could yield. Continued observation of the bridge excavation did not produce any further remains.

The raised coffin had an internal length of 1.83m and a width of about 0.42m; its surviving depth was about 0.26m. Pieces of eleven boards were present. Careful sieving of the remaining soil in the coffin produced fragments of three teeth, probably from a 30- to 40-year-old male, identified by local dentist Derek Mould. The base of the coffin retained the impression of a skeleton. The boards of the coffin had been lapped against each other and secured with nails. After freeze-drying at the Ancient Monuments Laboratory, London, the coffin returned to Lincoln in the 1990s and was briefly displayed. The author thanks Mick Clark and Naomi Field for their help with this discovery at different stages.

RE-USING CEMETERIES OF VANISHED MEDIEVAL CHURCHES

Rob Wheeler

> *Filthy place!*
> *Curious people!*
> *Bury their dead on top of the steeple*

This is not a reference to Lincoln but to Dartford in Kent, where overcrowding in the town's main churchyard led to the ground around a disused chapel being brought into use. The chapel sat above the steep valley in which the town was confined, so the burials were indeed above the top of the steeple. The example serves to remind us that disused churches could offer a solution to the overcrowding of urban burial grounds. Lincoln had lost something like 30 of its medieval churches: does that mean there was that number of potential additional burial grounds?

It was quite easy for a church to fall into disuse, or even to collapse physically, without affecting the use of the churchyard for burials. St Nicholas's church in Newport offered such an example in 1826, as White's Directory explained, when only the tower of the church survived but the churchyard continued to serve the parish and a minister preached a sermon there once a year in order to qualify for his stipend. The burial service would be read over the open grave, which was quite normal at the time: having a funeral service inside the church with addresses, etc., is a more modern development.

Much the same was true in the later middle ages. The church of St Peter-at-the-pump (otherwise known as St Peter *ad fontem*) just east of Rosemary Lane had as its patron the monastery of St Mary, York, whose cell just east of Lincoln is still known as Monks' Abbey. The monastery had been allowed to take the revenues from the church on condition that it appointed a vicar to look after it. The suburb east of Broadgate became so depopulated and the revenues of the church so small that in 1461 this condition was dropped: the Prior at Monks' Abbey was to carry out duties there himself or by a deputy. In 1542, when the remains of the church were taken down, it was recorded that the graveyard was looked after by one of the monks. The implication is that, even though the church was in ruins, at least occasional burials were continuing.

So we might expect that Lincoln in the early nineteenth century had lots of ancient cemeteries that could be brought into use. But what happened in Lincoln in the mid-sixteenth century was not a natural process of decay but the suppression of existing parishes. The city, having seen King Henry VIII's intentions towards the monasteries, was anxious to get its hands

St Martin's New Cemetery (Park Street/Beaumont Fee). (*Rob Wheeler*).

on church property in Lincoln that could be seen as serving no useful purpose: specifically, the materials of disused churches. It made a start in 1533, in an opportunistic manner. It may have paused when the Lincolnshire Rising showed just how strongly the populace felt about such matters. From what happens next, it seems to have run into opposition from the patrons of some of the churches, who no doubt felt that their own rights were being ignored. This led to the city obtaining an Act of Parliament in 1549 for the Union of Parishes.

The Act's declared intention was to form united parishes whose income would be sufficient to support an educated minister, well able to nurture the Reformed faith. It took care to preserve the rights of the suppressed churches' patrons, remaining close to what happened in a 'normal' union. By implication the rights of parishioners with regard to the graveyards (not explicitly mentioned in the Act) might be expected to follow 'normal' practice. The Corporation was granted powers to apply the materials of the suppressed churches to repair of other churches, to bridges and to the poor. That last provision could be interpreted very widely.

The final details of what was to happen under the Act were not formally settled until 1553, by which time Queen Mary was on the throne, but seem to have been acted on from a couple of years earlier. These arrangements rode roughshod over the rights of patrons – but perhaps only where the adjustments were between members of the Chapter. They did not explicitly harm the burial rights of parishioners or of the owners of monuments, but it is clear that,

The south wall of St Cuthbert's churchyard in Danes Terrace. (*Rob Wheeler*).

barring certain exceptions, those rights were to be ignored. The main exceptions concern St Mary Crackpole and St Cuthbert. Those are exactly the two cemeteries which in the first half of the nineteenth century were used to relieve pressure on existing burial grounds.

Thus it seems that, rather than having 30 ancient burial grounds available, the city actually had just two, and it did indeed use them.

There was resistance at St Andrew-in-Wigford where the Sutton family brought a Chancery suit. It would seem that there were tomb chests to members of the family and there had probably also been a chantry, now dissolved. Perhaps the lawyers started by arguing that the chantry chapel was a private construction, and it became clear that any claim based on a chantry was almost certain to fail. So the lawyers advanced the assertion that the whole church was a private chapel belonging to the Sutton family and not a parish church at all. That claim seems implausible; perhaps it was intended as an opening gambit that would lead to a compromise. In fact, they lost their case entirely. There may have been bigger issues at play. St Andrew's had housed chantries for The Great Gild of St Mary and the Gild of St Anne, which had been the two dominant bodies in the religious life of the lower city. One wonders whether the church had become a focus for maintenance of the old ways and resistance to Reform, and whether the puritan party on the Council saw its obliteration as essential to the godly cause.

The south-east corner of St Cuthbert's churchyard wall in Danes Terrace. (*Rob Wheeler*).

What happened elsewhere was complicated by the city gaining authority over the fabric of the churches, whilst the site became the property of the patron: sometimes the patron of the united parish – the Cathedral's Precentor seems to have done particularly well out of this – but when one of the canons had been patron of the previous church he often retained the site as part of his perquisites. Thus in 1552 the fabric of St John the Evangelist (opposite the Cornhill) had been sold to an alderman on condition that he built a good dwelling house towards the street, but the street frontage did not belong to the Corporation, so nothing seems to have been done. Likewise, at the Great Gowts, the Corporation granted the fabric of Holy Rood church to the Clothworkers' Guild so that they could establish a dye-house there, in the hope of creating extra employment. They were to have the churchyard for their *tenters* for stretching out the drying cloth 'if they could get it'.

The limits of the city's powers are made explicit when they established a committee to 'view and sell all the Bells, leade, tyle, tymber and other things that belong to any church that is or shalbe taken down within this city' and to enquire 'what persons have taken or purloyned anything lately belonging to the same churches that was not sold to them'. This needs to be borne in mind in reading an earlier order that headstones were not to be burned for lime. To a modern reader, this conjures up pictures of churchyards being cleared of their gravestones. However, the local limestone is unsuitable for creating the type of headstone we are accustomed to see in graveyards. Besides, such headstones (had they existed) would have remained the property of whoever erected them and their descendants. The order probably concerns the richer parishioners who had paid to be buried inside the church and where limestone slabs had been laid over the grave, forming part of the floor of the church, and incorporating an inscription at the head of the grave.

Increasing the area available for burials is unlikely to have been a concern of the men who drafted the 1549 Act and the 1553 order. It is noticeable that they only authorised the continued use of St Mary Crackpole and St Cuthbert's churchyards for residents of those late parishes. It seems likely that a family of some influence in each of those parishes had made a fuss about wanting to be buried with their forefathers. Such concerns are likely to have died away within a generation or so. By the late eighteenth century, when it becomes possible to inspect leases of these two churchyards, there is nothing to suggest that they were any different from the other ex-churchyards that belonged to prebends (i.e. to particular canons) at the cathedral. There is certainly no mention of continuing burials.

As it happens, St Martin's (which had gained St Mary Crackpole) and St Michael-on-the-Mount (which had gained St Cuthbert) were parishes that saw a particularly steep rise in population in the early nineteenth century. It was St Martin's that saw the first development. In 1820, the existing lease was surrendered and the Prebendary of St Mary Crackpole granted a new one, not to the parish of St Martin but to seven of its most notable inhabitants who would hold the land in trust 'to allow interment of all such Christians as may be entitled to burial in the said parish of St Martin'. It seems likely that the intention behind this arrangement was to give non-conformists complete equality of treatment with Anglicans in the use of the burial ground. The trustees were responsible for keeping the boundary walls in repair; perhaps the original idea was that they should charge fees and act as a sort of burial board. However, an entry in the 1822 churchwardens' accounts recording a payment for eight days' labour at 'the New Church Yard' suggests that, in practice, the management was left to the parish authorities.

The financial arrangements are something of a mystery. The holder of the previous lease must have been bought out, but did the Rev. H.V. Bayley, as Prebendary, charge a premium for granting the new lease or was it *gratis*? Edmund Venables, writing almost 70 years later, suggests the latter, and it does seem a coincidence that the two medieval churchyards that were brought into use in the nineteenth century happened to be those where continuing use was specified in the 1553 order. Had someone threatened to exercise that right of burial? If a funeral procession made its way to what was then just a paddock or a garden, would anyone have the nerve to stop an interment? It would reflect badly on the prebendary (and the non-conformists would doubtless take delight in the prebendary's embarrassment). This is not to suggest that any such event actually happened: an oblique allusion to the *possibility* of it happening might be enough to ensure cooperation by the prebendary.

Whilst there are gaps in our knowledge of what happened to St Mary Crackpole's churchyard, our ignorance about St Cuthbert's is almost total. It was still described as an ex-churchyard in 1828; by 1842 it was St Michael's new burial ground. So the change probably took place in the 1830s. A house had already been built in the north-west corner of the old churchyard and this remained. New boundary walls were built, and these can still be seen.

The revival of these medieval churchyards was short-lived. The sanitary movement had a horror of burials taking place in graveyards that were surrounded by urban bustle. This seems to have been driven less by scientific concerns about drainage and more by a pseudo-scientific belief that decomposing corpses would generate a harmful miasma that needed to be dispersed by the wind. It led to an Order in Council prohibiting burials after 1 November 1855 in almost all the existing burial grounds. This necessitated new burial grounds outside the urban area in the second half of the nineteenth century, which are examined in later chapters on the cemeteries at Canwick Road.

St Clement-in-the-Bail

Naomi Field

Wickham Gardens is a small park tucked away on the north-western side of Chapel Lane behind the Westgate Water Tower built in 1911. The gardens, donated to the city in 1914, included the city reservoir, which was constructed in around 1851, and which was later used as a public swimming baths. A bowling green and pond followed by 1930, and a play area by the 1960s. In 2008, City of Lincoln Council was considering an option to sell the site for development and commissioned Lindsey Archaeological Services to undertake an archaeological evaluation. A fuller report on the excavations by Rubén López Catalán was prepared at the time on which the results of the excavation in this chapter is based. It was hoped that evidence might be found for the elusive parish church of St Clement-in-the-Bail, the least well known of the Bail churches.

The dedication to St Clement was popular amongst the Danish elite who became established in England after the accession of Cnut in 1014, suggesting that the church had been a pre-Conquest foundation, possibly starting life as a private chapel, before becoming a parish church. It was one of four churches that are known to have existed in the upper city

before the Norman Conquest, situated in each of the quadrants of the Roman Upper City. David Stocker has suggested that they each belonged to one of the four principal lords, St Clement's most likely to the Sheriff. Although mention of the church itself does not occur in documents until 1302, documents related to properties said to be within the parish occur from the later twelfth century. Pottery of early-mid eleventh century date was found at nearby sites, indicating that this area was occupied before the Conquest, and St Paul-in-

A cist burial in front of wall foundation, looking south. (*Naomi Field*).

the-Bail was long established by then. It may have ceased to function as a parish by the late fourteenth century but the cemetery remained defined until at least 1457. While the church is not marked on J.S. Padley's series of city maps published between 1842 and 1883, its suggested location is shown on the Ordnance Survey 1:500 scale map of 1887 and in subsequent OS editions up to 1930. It was identified as sitting west of the bend in Chapel Lane and on the 1930 map, due east of the water tower, beneath what is now 51 Chapel Lane, as shown on more recent maps.

In 2008, seven trenches were excavated across Wickham Gardens. One of them, an inverted 'L'-shaped trench, was dug inside the south-east corner of the former bowling green and just north-east of the water

tower. Beneath a layer of rubble, a heavily robbed-out limestone wall aligned north-south, crossed the middle of the trench. A series of pits had later been dug, possibly to rob the walls or for collecting stone for lime-burning is not known, with pottery from the end of the fourteenth century or later. The same rubble deposit abutted a second robbed-out wall, aligned east-west in the southern arm of the trench, with another layer of rubble sealing the robbed-out wall.

Between the two walls were two stone-lined cist burials also sealed by the lower layer of demolition rubble. They were less than two metres apart. They were left *in*

Wall foundation in front of a cist burial, looking west. (*Naomi Field*).

situ and not excavated although the cover slabs had become dislodged revealing the bones inside the cists, confirming their function. Although no direct dating evidence was recovered from the burials they are similar to medieval burials found in other Lincoln cemeteries, for example at The Lawn (St Bartholomew's) during excavations between 1984 and 1987, and also at St Mark's church, excavated in 1976. Further examples have been recorded beyond the city limits and are known to be generally of the tenth- to twelfth-century date.

While the excavations were limited in extent the association of the robbed-out walls with the two graves suggests that they may have been the remains of the lost church of St Clement-in-the-Bail, perhaps representing the north wall of a tower and west wall of the nave of a church. Alternatively, they could represent the south and east walls of a nave, which would mean the graves lay inside the church. The limited associated dating of the pits cutting one of the walls is in keeping with the documentary evidence that indicates the church fell into disuse by the late fourteenth century.

Graves at St Katherine's Priory

Colin Brown

The area of the city known as St Catherine's is named after the Gilbertine priory of St Katherine's that used to be situated west of St Catherine's and the Fosse Way and close to its junction with Cross o'Cliff Hill. The former church of St Katherine's, opened in 1887, lies to the north.

The Gilbertines were the only purely English religious order, founded by a Lincolnshire priest, Gilbert. He established a monastery at Sempringham in c. 1131, initially for a small community of nuns, but eventually to include canons as well. At the time of the Dissolution of the monasteries under Henry VIII, the order was able to boast some 26 religious houses. St Katherine's itself was established by Bishop Robert de Chesney shortly after 1148.

In 2007 part of the eastern side of the priory complex was excavated prior to residential development of two former Victorian properties fronting on to St Catherines. The area excavated measured approximately 180 m^2, and yielded important new information exposing

The west side of the cemetery, looking south west, with six bodies in the foreground. (*Colin Brown*).

several phases of cemetery and building remains associated with the priory complex. Some 56 graves containing human remains were investigated which significantly could be broadly linked with specific events relating to the history and structural development of the priory.

The earliest cemetery was probably associated with the origins of the priory with associated finds being dated to around the mid-twelfth century. Twelve graves were investigated, and displayed a remarkable uniformity, with each burial being within a relatively sophisticated stone cist, eleven incorporating head niches. All the individuals were young prime adult males, and it has been suggested that these men were most likely high-status benefactors of the monastery. For this early phase, there were no clearly associated structural remains, other than a few post holes that were difficult to interpret.

At some point between the mid-twelfth to thirteenth centuries, an apsidal building was constructed, apparently ecclesiastical in form, much of which lay beyond the west side of the excavation. Parts of this building had cut through the burials described above. Twenty-

A body in a stone cist. (*Colin Brown*).

two graves have been linked, to the life of this structure, including seven in slightly less sophisticated cists. The skeletons within these were all adult, and mostly male (four were female, and two could not be sexed). These individuals also probably paid for the privilege of being buried within a priory cemetery, which at this time would not have been open to all. They may have been middle-ranking benefactors, possibly even family members of the order.

The apsidal chapel was eventually dismantled, some time during the thirteenth and fourteenth centuries to make way for a significantly larger, possibly rectangular, structure at a time when the wool trade, the principal economic turbine of the priory, was still flourishing. This new building may have been relatively short-lived, as its truncated remains were sealed beneath an accumulated deposit that incorporated finds of broadly fifteenth- to sixteenth-century date. It has been speculated that this deposit, coupled with the absence of any renewed structural activity, could reflect wider trends associated, for example, with the devastating effects of the Bubonic Plague, and/or a general decline in the wool trade, upon which the priory economy was so heavily dependent. Possibly, thereafter, full recovery was not viable.

There was, however, renewed burial activity evidenced by 22 burials within the excavated area; mostly again males, but also five females and one infant; an indication that the wider community, and not just benefactors of the priory, were now able to be laid to rest within this, by now quite ancient, burial ground.

St Katherine's eventually met the same fate as other English monasteries: dissolution under Henry VIII in July 1538, after which the locally important Grantham family are known to have converted the priory buildings into secular mansions. The post-dissolution archaeology was indicated within the excavated area only as an abandonment/dereliction horizon, up to 75cm thick in places.

The Burial Ground of the Medieval Jewish Community

Chris Johnson

Medieval Lincoln was home to a sizeable community of Jews, who seem to have settled in the city in the years following the civil war between Stephen and Matilda. The community, which numbered several hundred at its peak in the early thirteenth century, formed a significant sector of the city's population, and from available sources are known to have inhabited at least 70 properties in the area extending from the Bail as far south as the Wigford suburb.

Their burial ground was probably established in the period after 1177, before which it was the custom to inter their remains in a central cemetery in London. The location for the Lincoln burial ground has never been identified, and we know of it only from a few records dating from the period of the expulsion of the Jews from the whole country, which took place in 1290. Their cemetery was listed in that year in a schedule of Jewish properties drawn up for purposes of selling them off, valued at just 3s. 6d.. It remained unsold for whatever

Possible site of the medieval Jewish cemetery, now part of Liquorice Park, near Yarborough Road. (*Andrew Walker*).

reason until 1293 when Walter of Carlisle, a Lincoln goldsmith with other properties in the north and west of the city, bought the site for 40 shillings. He died at some point between 1299 and 1317, and we do not know who inherited it.

As to the location of this burial ground, it is possible to narrow down the search. For one thing, Lincoln would probably have followed the general practice of having the Jewish cemetery situated outside the city walls, but in an area readily accessible to the community. In Oxford, for example it was just outside the eastern wall. Norwich was the exception as the site there was well within the city walls. On the eastern side of Lincoln, the suburb of Butwerk and the area towards the east were already well developed, and most of the area to the north of Newport suburb was given over to stone quarries and open fields belonging to the citizens. The south side was also heavily occupied and available land was very limited. This leaves the western suburbs to consider, and it seems that the slope from what is now Carline Road down towards the modern-day Carholme Road may possibly have been suitable, as well as fairly accessible for mourners coming from the main areas of the Jewish population.

Interestingly there is a late sixteenth-century reference to a property called 'Paradise', which lay within the area just suggested, but there is no hope of taking this name further back in time. All trace of burials and any memorial stones (evidence for which has been found elsewhere) have long since disappeared, maybe erased, soon after the expulsion.

Lincoln Friends' Burial Ground
Erin Bell

The burial ground of the Religious Society of Friends (Quakers), between Beaumont Fee and Park Street, is no longer visible. By the early twentieth century, much of it was covered by an extension to the original, late seventeenth-century, Meeting House. Changing uses of the land, originally set aside for burials in the 1660s, mirrored the experiences of Lincoln Quakers, initially reflecting a need to legitimise a religious minority and protect interments from attack, to Friends' acceptance in the late nineteenth century that land in which Quakers were buried might be used to benefit the city's living.

Prior to the founding of the burial ground in 1668, Friends buried their dead in fields and orchards, although in 1668 they became concerned to secure land specifically for that purpose, which was especially important for a group originating in the tumultuous Civil War and Interregnum, who sought to survive the Restoration in part by visibly rejecting the violent disorder of earlier decades. Lincolnshire's Quakers were certainly keen to fence off burial grounds, perhaps to mark them out for future generations – to 'Remaine Certaine to Posterity' as required by Lincolnshire Quarterly Meeting, which gathered every few months with representatives of smaller Monthly Meetings.

This guaranteed a demarcated site in which Friends from specific Meetings could be interred. This was not dependent on 'the will [of] one' Friend to allow burials on their land, and instead was 'setled to Friends of the whole Meeting'. It also served the organisational purpose of reminding Friends, even as meetings moved, grew, and in later years dwindled and sometimes closed, where remains of the faithful lay. This may, especially in the Restoration era, have legitimised Quakers in the eyes of others, by offering an orderly equivalent to Anglican cemeteries, and limiting the risk of anti-Quaker attacks, but not always successfully. In 1685, according to Gainsborough Monthly Meeting, a Magistrate ordered the removal of fencing at 'Tanby' [Thealby] burial ground, leaving it 'open and exposed to the Beasts, or to the Rudeness of Persons more inhuman, usually attending on such mischievous Occasions.'

Certainly, Quakers faced criticism owing to their distinctiveness. For example, Quaker burials were different from those of other Christians, most notably because Friends did not have clergy; rather ministers might travel the country but were not attached to one Meeting and men or women might fulfil this role. Although burials were not led by a priest, an elder, considered significant in their faith, might guide the family, whilst the whole meeting determined who could be buried. Friends do not seem to have been harsh in their response to requests and young children who could not be determined as yet Quaker were often buried in such sites at their parents' request.

After its foundation, Lincoln burial ground was in regular use from the 1670s, when ten of the first Quakers were laid to rest, followed by nine more in the 1680s, including several who lived outside Lincoln but were part of Gainsborough Monthly Meeting, of which Lincoln Meeting was part. Others, especially before the 1689 Toleration Act, were gaoled for their faith and some died in Lincoln Gaol in appalling conditions, leading to burial in the Quaker burial ground: John Titmos of Moulton, yeoman and member of Spalding Monthly Meeting, died in 1680, having refused to pay church rates, and was buried in Lincoln. In addition, analysis of Friends' accounts of their 'sufferings', oppression by authorities for failure to engage with the Anglican church, suggests an additional burial: Mary Waterman of Stegnes [Skegness] died in April 1687 while imprisoned in Lincoln Castle for nonpayment of tithes, a tax on household income demanded by the Anglican church. Kept in 'a Smoaky Room [where] she grew weaker and weaker', she was likely buried in Lincoln rather than being transferred to the coast.

The Toleration Act meant that dissenting Protestants were free to worship without punishment. In practical terms, Friends could hope to meet without persecution, and funded a Meeting House rather than relying on surreptitious gatherings in members' houses.

The Friends' Meeting House, 1689. (*Erin Bell*).

Using land already held, Friends had a Meeting House built on the burial ground, possibly over existing graves. Although burials dating from the 1670s would have been within living memory, graves would not necessarily have been marked, so it may have been difficult to keep track of their precise location. Furthermore, details of attacks on Quaker burial grounds elsewhere in the county may have led to a decision to build over known graves to protect them in a period when the extent of support for Toleration amongst former antagonists was not clear. However, this cannot be proved.

Certainly, though, the 1689 Meeting House *was* built within the burial ground, and Friends continued to meet regularly until the mid-eighteenth century, by which point so few Friends lived locally that the Monthly Meeting moved to Brant Broughton and a cobbler paid rent on a building within the burial ground. Lincoln's star had risen again by the early nineteenth century when abolitionism and psychiatric care became of growing importance to Quakers and the Meeting House offered a central venue for speakers, for which the approval of Lincoln Corporation, some of whom, as Susan Davies notes, were anti-abolitionist, was not formally required. Therefore, a drop in burials can be charted in the eighteenth century, with roots in the limited use of the Meeting House. Burials dwindled from around nine or ten per decade in the 1670s and 1680s to six in the 1690s and two in 1700–29. The next cluster reflects a return to use of the Meeting House in the early nineteenth century, with seven burials between 1801 and 1837, the final one, a five-week-old baby, Alfred Fieldsend of Broughton and Gainsborough.

It is possible to collate details of 34 burials, from Lincolnshire Quarterly Meeting's records, plus Mary Waterman. However, wills survive for several Quakers buried in Lincoln as well as non-Quaker family members, giving a sense of the status of those buried in the late seventeenth and early eighteenth centuries as well as their wider kin. John Aystrop, for example, was buried in December 1689 and described as a yeoman, a landholder with a small estate, who lived in Brackleby [Brattleby]. He was interred in 'the burying place at Lincolne', bequeathing his three daughters £30 each at adulthood, with the remainder to his wife. Nathaniel Greg[g], another yeoman, husband of Elizabeth and father of Esther, mentioned Elizabeth in his 1675 will (Esther may not yet have been born), although he may not have been Quaker as there is no record of a burial after his will was proved in 1675, three years before his wife and daughter's burials in the burial ground. His support for his Quaker wife suggests grassroots toleration in a decade notorious for persecution of religious minorities, which may have been more likely in rural areas outside the Anglican stronghold. Those buried in the city but living in villages had rural occupations and experienced less persecution than their co-religionists.

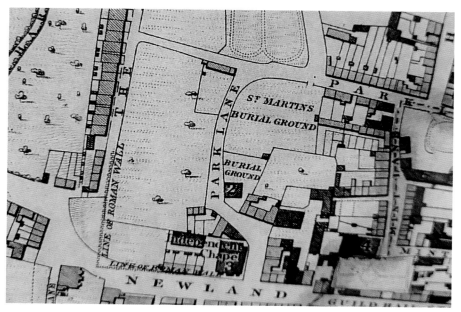

Map of the Friends' Meeting House and burial ground, located immediately south of St Martin's burial ground, as represented on J. S. Padley's 1851 map. (*Source: D.R. Mills and R.C. Wheeler, eds,* Historic Town Plans of Lincoln, 1610–1920, *2004, p. 64*).

Use of the burial ground had begun to dwindle again by the 1830s, reflecting lessening use of the Meeting House for worship, as opposed to educational activities, a decline in Quaker numbers nationally, and the worsening state of the building. Its closure, though, was in response to an 1855 Act of Parliament to regulate and limit burials in urban areas to 'protect the public health', and ended almost two centuries of use. Along with decreasing use of the Meeting House, this led in 1875 to an offer by the Lincoln Corporation to buy the Meeting House and remaining burial ground to widen the road. The minutes of Monthly Meetings reveal that a committee was set up 'on the sale of the Meeting House', and had met the mayor and corporation, although it was determined that the property needed to be valued. When a sum of £750 was suggested by Friends, the Corporation asked to buy the strip of land next to the Meeting House for £10, 'for the alternation and improvement of the street', perhaps in response to a petition of 1868 by inhabitants regarding the poor condition of roads. This was agreed, although the land formed part of the original burial ground and it is not clear if Friends discussed the likelihood of burials within it. Perhaps it was known not to have been used. If this was not certain, it may suggest a pragmatic approach by Quakers, balancing the fate of human remains against the potential to improve the city. This was not without precedent; Chris Skidmore notes a similar situation in Reading some decades earlier, when the burial ground was in regular use.

As the condition of the Meeting House continued to worsen, Friends in the early twentieth century began to consider the possibility of building a new Meeting House. Today referred to as the 1910 Room, at its inception it was seen as a new place of worship, with residual funds used to improve the original building. Quaker records reveal that Friends knew that the planned building work possibly lay over existing graves. The Monthly Meeting minutes of November 1908 noted that 'the building [would be] over the graveyard.' However, owing to earlier Quaker *mores*, their precise locations would have been difficult to determine. Yearly Meeting, a business meeting for all British Quakers, ordered headstones to be removed from burial grounds in 1717, originating in later seventeenth- and eighteenth-century plain testimony, a rejection of excessive consumption. This was rescinded only in 1850, at which point there had been no Quaker burials in Lincoln for more than a decade. Ultimately, the 1910 Meeting House was built adjacent to the 1689 building, on a section of burial ground which certainly included unmarked graves from 1717–1837 and potentially older interments, and was officially opened in October 1910, as reported both in the *Lincolnshire Echo* and in the national Quaker periodical, *The Friend*, likely alerted by a circular from the Monthly Meeting Building Committee earlier that month. *The Friend* commented favourably and, in practical terms, noted it was 'on part of the graveyard at the rear'. Corporation planning records for the new building are not extant, and it is not clear if Friends debated the decision to build on the burial ground; it may have been viewed as a fitting way to mark earlier Friends' graves, or otherwise acceptable because of the potential of the building work to help maintain Quakerism in the city for future centuries.

Maps of the city, and specifically of the area around Beaumont Fee and Park Street, help in tracking the changing shape of the Meeting House and therefore the size and shape of the remaining, visible burial ground. An 1851 map by J.S. Padley shows the area behind the Meeting House (to the east) as an arboreal site, with a 1930 Ordnance Survey map depicting the 1910 building taking up the majority of the remaining burial ground and underlining the extent to which both Meeting Houses had, by 1910, left little of the original site empty. It seems unlikely that the majority of graves lie elsewhere than under the Meeting Houses, or perhaps the strip sold in 1875. The level of cartographical detail, even in Ordnance Survey maps, is also misleading: Friends' burial ground is rarely identified as such. St Martin's burial ground behind it is often marked, however, potentially leading to misidentification of it as Quaker.

In conclusion, Friends' burial ground lies under the 1910 Meeting House, as Friends at the time remarked, but also the 1689 post-Toleration Meeting House and the garden in front of it, the car park to its rear and the strip of land sold to the Corporation. Graves almost certainly lie under the 1910 building and likely other areas. As unusual as this may seem, it is in keeping with plain testimony, with unmarked graves preserved under a place of worship, and possibly also under sites of benefit to living inhabitants, in keeping with Friends' initially self-protective, later philanthropic, aspirations.

The Churchyard of St Paul-in-the-Bail

Lesley Church

The church of St Paul-in-the-Bail stood for centuries, on the site of the Roman forum, at the junction of Bailgate and Westgate, though there was a succession of different church buildings over those centuries. The last of the sequence, which was built in 1877–9 to a design by A.W. Blomfield, was demolished in 1971 and archaeological excavations took place on the site over the following years. The site of the former church is now a much-used open space. Some gravestones from the churchyard remain, laid as paving. Archaeological evidence suggests that there were burials on the site from as early as the seventh century.

A wall enclosed the Victorian church and churchyard. In living memory, the gravestones were confined to the east of the church interspersed with trees and shrubs and a hedge around the low wall from which the iron railings had been removed during the Second World War. A pathway led from Bailgate through the gravestones and between the south wall of the church and a triangle of grass, which once could also have been part of the graveyard, to the entrance to the church facing Westgate.

A picture by the Swiss artist Samuel Hieronymus Grimm of the Georgian church, which preceded Blomfield's, shows the headstones surrounding the modest building. By the 1800s the churchyard must have been becoming overcrowded. Until 1800, paupers who died in the House of Industry, west of the castle, were buried in the churchyard at St Paul's, as it was the nearest parish church. In that year the vestry informed the directors of the House of Industry that the church could only take burials of inmates who had formerly been parishioners, and others had to be interred in their own parishes. In 1800, there were 32 burials at St Paul's, and of these 21 were residents of the House of Industry. In 1827, the situation had become worse and the vestry resolved that no burials at all were to be received within the churchyard from the House of Industry or from the Lunatic Asylum (now The Lawn) which had opened in 1819 on land to the south of the House of Industry. Both these institutions had to make other arrangements. The directors of the House of Industry set aside a portion of their own land for use as a cemetery. When a new Union Workhouse was planned for Lincoln in 1837, which superseded the House of Industry, the Directors offered three acres of land adjoining their burial ground as a site for the new workhouse, at a cost of £650. The offer was accepted and the workhouse was built on this land to the north of the House of Industry between Burton Road and Upper Long Leys Road. The workhouse had its own burial ground to its west. Nigel Horner's chapter examines these institutions and the arrangements they made to bury their dead.

There were occasionally burials in St Paul's churchyard of patients from the hospital at the top of Michaelgate and prisoners from the Castle. Notably, one young man from Gainsborough,

Site of St Paul-in-the-Bail, looking east. (*Lesley Church*).

Thomas Knapton, a marine aged 17, was hanged for rape at Cobb Hall in August 1833. The jury had recommended leniency on account of his youth but the judge had disagreed. The hanging would have been visible from the churchyard and may well have been watched from there by some of the large crowd that had gathered. Afterwards, Thomas's friends took his body to St Paul's churchyard for burial the same day.

From the 1840s, finding space in the churchyard for a new influx of burials must have caused the churchwardens at St Paul-in-the-Bail further concern. Castle Dykings starts to appear as 'Abode' for many of the entries in the burial register. This huddle of squalid, though recently built, houses – described by the newspapers as a 'den of iniquity' – at the corner of Westgate and Union Road close to 'The Strugglers Inn', was extra-parochial, but St Paul's was the nearest church.

Full churchyards were a problem throughout the city and, from the 1840s, there was discussion on the need for new burial grounds. In some churchyards it was impossible to

Site of St Paul-in-the-Bail, looking west. (*Lesley Church*).

dig a new grave without disturbing previous interments, and this must surely have been the case at St Paul's churchyard. Conditions in these urban graveyards were insanitary and liable to spread disease. However, no action was taken in Lincoln until the Burial (Beyond the Metropolis) Act of 1853 came into force, which stated that burials in cities and towns in churchyards were to be discontinued from November 1855, and that burial boards, made up of representatives of parishes, were to be set up to investigate and provide alternative solutions. These new cemeteries are considered elsewhere in chapters by Arthur Ward and Andrew Walker

The churchyard at St Paul-in-the-Bail was certainly part of the 'active life' of the area. It was located at one of the busiest parts of the uphill city since Roman times and the area was becoming increasingly populous in the nineteenth century. By then, the church was set amidst shops, workshops, butchers' slaughter houses, stables, and numerous public houses. The churchyard may not always have been treated with the respect the churchwardens would have liked. The church wall was liable to damage from the traffic at the narrow junction of

Bailgate with Westgate. Fowls and animals from neighbouring properties could wander into the churchyard. In 1811, the town crier was paid 6d to announce that washing should no longer be spread out to dry in the churchyard.

The Georgian church of St Paul-in-the-Bail, built in 1786 to replace the previous church which had stood there from 1301, was too small for the growing population of the parish by 1877, and it was decided to demolish the church and rebuild on the site. The new larger church must have covered some of the areas of the earlier churchyard and involved the removal of gravestones. This Victorian church served the parish until the 1960s when dwindling congregations caused the Church Commissioners to authorise demolition and the parish of St Paul-in-the-Bail amalgamated with St Mary Magdalene. The last rector of St Paul's Church was the Rev. Ernest Milton who left Lincoln in 1964. His *The Church and Parish of St Paul-in-the-Bail Lincoln* (Lincoln, 1946) is a valuable resource for the history of the churches now long gone.

In 1971 the church awaited demolition. As the *Lincolnshire Echo* commented on 14 October 1971: 'For almost six years, the 19th century church has stood closed and shuttered – the once well-kept garden now rambling and overgrown.'

Places of Rest Within Welfare Institutions

Nigel Horner

According to Keith Snell in his book *Parish and Belonging*, graveyards and cemeteries are symbolic places of belonging, of status, and of social standing, where the community affords dignity and respect to the deceased, and their family, through the ritual of a standard Christian burial within the bounds of parish cemeteries and graveyards. That said, a number of those less fortunate in their lives, and in their deaths, have been thought of as being beyond the pale, beyond respectability, and have thus been excluded from these facilities.

Such persons are those who have breathed their last within institutions, including the Lincoln Union Workhouse on Burton Road, the Lincoln County Hospital on Drury Lane, St Anne's Bede Houses, on Sewell Road, and the Lincoln Lunatic Asylum (latterly known as The Lawn Hospital) on Union Road.

Lincoln Union Workhouse – founded 1796; rebuilt 1837
For some residents who died in the Lincoln workhouse, the graveyard adjoining upper Long Leys Road was their final resting place. This plot was significantly enlarged in 1828, when diocesan records reported 'an Act of Consecration and Dedication of a piece of land belonging to the Directors of the Poor … for a Burial Place of persons dying in the House of Industry'. Under the provisions of the Poor Law Act of 1834, a new workhouse was built three years later to the south of Burton Road and to the west of the Lincoln Lunatic Asylum. Costing £11,000, and designed by W.A. Nicholson, it was intended to house 360 'paupers'.

From the minute books, it is apparent that undertakers for the poor were appointed by contract. Among them was one William Bescoby, who, in 1828, supplied coffins at 12s. a piece. The cost of this was altered in 1831 to 14s. for paupers aged 12 or above, and 5s. for those under that age.

Some information about the House of Industry burial ground can be gleaned from newspaper accounts of an alleged case of body-snatching which occurred there in 1829. According to a report in *Drakard's Stamford News* on 19 June 1829, the governor of the House of Industry, whilst on a daily walk, looked over the walls of the cemetery and noticed that a grave, which had been dug ten days earlier, had been disturbed. The report shed some light on the burial practice relating to this unfortunate inmate, 65-year-old John Hardy. It noted that the coffin was disturbed, though the funeral shroud and evergreens were left behind. Parts of the body were found in Monks Lane; the 'intestines, back and belly' were found buried near the House of Industry, though, at the time of writing, it was stated in the report that the head

The burial ground can be seen to the west of the workhouse buildings on this J. S. Padley map of 1883. (*Source: D.R. Mills and R.C. Wheeler, eds, Historic Town Plans of Lincoln, 1610–1920, 2004, p. 89*).

and legs had not been discovered. Several months later, Thomas Johnson, a young medical student was charged with taking the dead body of a pauper from the burial-ground of the House of Industry. He was not convicted.

Generally, little is known about those interred in the workhouse burial ground. However, one person buried there as a pauper who did attract some attention was Peter Bishop. Born

The workhouse: the children's block from the north west in 1965. (*Courtesy of Lincoln Central Library, Lincolnshire County Council/GLL*).

in Barbados in circa 1792, he had enlisted in the 2nd battalion of 69th (South Lincolnshire) Regiment of Foot in 1806. He married Ann Powell at St.Swithin's Church in May 1810, and saw service as a drummer at the battle of Waterloo in 1815. After numerous periods of imprisonment, Peter Bishop was admitted to the workhouse with a recorded occupation of 'tramp'. The *Stamford Mercury*, of 11 July 1851 announced: 'Died in the Lincoln Union Workhouse, on Saturday last … Peter Bishop. Who had been known for many years in the city and neighbourhood as "Peter the Black", aged 65.'

By the end of 1856, the cemetery was further enlarged, and the diocesan records note that there was established in the parish of St Peter in Eastgate 'an additional cemetery or burial ground for the interment of the bodies of persons dying inmates of the Lincoln Union' on account of the 'present burial ground being insufficient'. The plot was bounded to the east by the workhouse garden, to the west by land then used as a burial ground 'for persons not members of the Church of England', to the north by the old burial ground, and to the south by a 'road leading from the said Workhouse grounds to the Workhouse Water Tank'.

As Adam Cartwright's chapter on undertakers has observed, there did seem to be some unfortunate economies made by those arranging the funerals of the poor. However, in an advertisement placed in the *Lincolnshire Chronicle* on 18 March 1884, W. B. Danby, the clerk to the Lincoln Union sought to ensure that those who died in the Lincoln Union workhouse were provided with a respectable interment. Contractors were invited to tender to supply elm coffins for paupers dying there. These were to be of at least three-quarter inch plank, well-pitched, thoroughly tight at the edges and to be lined with calico, having four strong handles with a plate giving the dead person's name, age and date of death, which was to be affixed to the lid. The successful contractor was also to arrange carriage of the body and coffin to the place of burial in a suitable 'well-springed' conveyance. For those bodies to be buried in the workhouse cemetery, it was stated that four bearers would be provided.

The later workhouse graveyard ceased to be used after 1899, being deemed full. There were several rather gruesome accounts of the overcrowding of the workhouse cemetery before this forced closure. From 1899 onwards, those who died in the workhouse were buried elsewhere in one of Lincoln's other cemeteries, usually at one of these on Canwick Road. Five years later, however, the workhouse cemetery was again in the news when it appeared to have been overrun by rats, who some commentators thought were feeding on the dead bodies. This was never proven.

The Old County Hospital, Drury Lane – opened 1777; closed 1878
Lincoln County Hospital was established by 'a meeting of Nobility, Gentry and Clergy of the County of Lincoln' in September 1768 which resolved:

> 1. 'That an Hospital for the Reception of the sick and sane Poor of this county will be of Publick Utility'; 2. 'that Lincoln is the most proper place in the County for that Purpose'; and 3. 'That a Committee ... be desired ... to prepare Rules and Orders for the Government of such Hospital'.

The first Hospital opened in a leased house in St Swithin's parish in November 1769, which was soon to be replaced by a purpose-built hospital in Drury Lane from 19 October 1777. This served as the Lincoln County Hospital until the new establishment was built on its current site on Greetwell Road in 1878.

The sale particulars for the Old County Hospital, Drury Lane (1887) clearly showed that the hospital had its own burial ground to the south west of the site, adjoining Gibraltar Hill. The plan also revealed that the dead house (or mortuary) was located on the corner of Drury Lane and Gibraltar Hill.

However, it is clear that 'since erection of the hospital those dying in hospital have been buried in the churchyard' (of St Michael on the Mount), such that in 1828 the space was enlarged as it 'is nearly filled up and will shortly become insufficient for the interment of the bodies of persons dying within the said parish'.

Site of burial ground linked to the old County Hospital. (*Nigel Horner*).

Workhouse burial ground, as seen from Upper Long Leys Road. (*Grace Timmins*).

St Anne's Bedehouses, Sewell Road – opened 1854

On 19 September 1854, there occurred an Act of Consecration and Dedication of the newly erected chapel and cemetery belonging to St Anne's Bedehouses. Designed by Augustus Welby Pugin, this set of 14 dwellings provided accommodation for 'females of limited resources, who were committed to the Church of England'. The benefactor of this scheme was the clergyman Richard Waldo Sibthorp, son of Col. Humphrey Waldo Sibthorp, Tory MP for Lincoln. He occupied the post of chaplain, and was warden until the end of 1864, whereupon he rejoined the Roman Catholic Church.

Such was Sibthorp's concern for the residents that plans for a chapel were drawn up once the dwellings were completed. Pugin's plans for the church were deemed unaffordable. Instead,

St Anne's Bedehouse chapel, 2006. (*Richard Croft*).

a somewhat more modest chapel was designed by William Butterfield, opening for services in June 1854 and consecrated three months later.

The adjoining graveyard provided a final resting place for deceased residents. At the time of the cemetery's consecration by the Bishop of Lincoln in September 1854, two of the Bedehouses' former inmates had already been buried there, in grounds on the north and east sides of the chapel which in a report of the consecration, the *Lincolnshire Chronicle* described as being laid out 'in exceedingly good taste'.

The Lincoln Lunatic Asylum (later known as The Lawn), Union Road – opened 1819

The Lincoln Lunatic Asylum was first proposed by resident physicians and surgeons at the County Hospital at the end of the eighteenth century and a first meeting to plan its development was held in 1800. From the outset, under the direction of Dr Edward Parker Charlesworth and Charles Cookson, the facility accommodated a mixture of 'pauper' patients paid for by subscribing parishes from across Lincolnshire, alongside some fee-paying residents.

Following the 1845 County Asylum Lunacy Act, the Lincolnshire Pauper Lunatic Asylum – subsequently known as St John's Hospital) was established at Bracebridge. On April 1855, a consecration and dedication of a new burial chapel and cemetery took place there. From its opening, those defined at the time as pauper lunatics were accommodated in the Bracebridge Heath facility rather than at The Lawn. As the diocesan records note 'since opening of said Asylum, the paupers that have died therein … have been buried in the churchyard of the Parish of Bracebridge'.

Whilst the steady growth of the asylum – and the death of its patients – would undoubtedly have created pressures of space on local graveyards, the overriding concern was to ensure that those excluded and marginalised in life should remain thus in death. With the Bracebridge Heath institution accommodating the poor from the mid-nineteenth century onwards, the vast majority of those housed at The Lawn were private patients. Following their deaths, families generally arranged for these patients' burials in family plots elsewhere, rather than allowing them the indignity of interment in the grounds of the asylum.

Memory and memorials
Some paupers were indeed taken away upon death by their relatives, from asylums, hospitals, and workhouses, to be buried in their originating parishes or resting places of choice. For many families, however, this expense was beyond their means and it was determined, shortly after setting up the Poor Law Unions, that the paupers' places of settlement, their parishes, should pay for the funeral wherever it took place.

The graveyard of the Lincoln Workhouse is overgrown, untended and impenetrable. What can be concluded is that the known are rightly and appropriately memorialised, whilst the unknown, the marginalised and the historically excluded, are discredited and effectively denied a memory. It is incumbent upon current and future curators to excavate these hidden histories.

The Lawn, Union Road. (*Andrew Walker*).

Newport Cemetery

Andrew Walker

The origins of the current Newport Cemetery can be traced back to 1855, when the St Nicholas and St John Burial Board was formed. The two parishes declined to join with nine of the others in the city in establishing the Canwick Road cemetery, instead wishing to continue to bury their dead uphill. Prior to the opening of the new cemetery, inhabitants of the two parishes were buried in their churchyards, despite the fact that the churches of St Nicholas and St John had long been demolished.

St Nicholas's churchyard was located on the corner of Newport and Church Lane, though the church of St Nicholas had been taken down in 1643 during the English Civil War. Despite there being no church, the benefice of St Nicholas continued, preserved by the preaching of an annual sermon in the churchyard. The church of St John the Baptist had been located near to the current site of Bishop Grosseteste University. It was demolished in 1545. The continued payment of parish clergy linked to these two parishes, despite there being no churches, caused much outcry. By the 1830s, the two rapidly growing parishes attracted much critical attention, becoming as one observer in the *Stamford Mercury* noted on 17 June 1831, 'the refuge for bad characters of every description.' Finally, the foundation stone of a new church in the parish of St Nicholas, on Newport, was laid in April 1839 and the building, the first parish church commission of renowned architect George Gilbert Scott, was consecrated by the Bishop of Lincoln in November 1840.

The new St Nicholas and St John Burial Board purchased nearly an acre of land from the county's sheriff for £152, near to the church of St Nicholas. A surveyor, W. Skill, was appointed and stonemasons and builders were hired to construct 'fence-walls, gates etc.'. Some £400 had been expended on its purchase and preparation. Part of the new cemetery was consecrated for Anglican use by the Bishop of Lincoln in December 1855; the unconsecrated ground was left for the use of other denominations.

As the population of uphill Lincoln expanded, so it became necessary for the cemetery to grow. Extensions were added in 1869, when again the Bishop of Lincoln was invited to consecrate some of the additional land for the interment of Anglicans. In 1898, a substantial addition was negotiated, with new ground of nearly three acres purchased from Colonel Willson. A year earlier, the architect William Scorer had been hired to enhance the design of the cemetery, with perimeter iron fencing being installed by W.G. Henton.

In 1913, now under the control of Lincoln Corporation rather than a burial board, a further 1.25 acres of land was purchased, and hopes were expressed in the *Lincolnshire Echo* of 5 December 1913 that a chapel and carriage drive would also be added. In 1925, the last

Gravediggers posing for the camera with the Cathedral in the background, c.1900. The many glass globes in evidence contained artificial flowers (known as *immortelles*) usually made of china or plaster of paris, bought from undertakers. These were fashionable grave objects at the time. (*Courtesy of Lincoln Central Library, Lincolnshire County Council/GLL. Ref. LCL832*).

substantial addition to the cemetery's grounds took place, with the addition of a further three acres, near the end of St John's Road, by which time the cemetery's area comprised over 25 acres, having been just over four acres in 1907. This was reported in an article in the *Lincolnshire Echo* on 1 July 1949, which noted that the city possessed just over 48 acres of burial grounds. At this time, therefore, Newport Cemetery constituted just over half of the city's interment space, and the newspaper report noted there was 'still plenty of space left'.

In addition to its extension, improvements had been made to the cemetery. In 1933, a new entrance to the cemetery was opened from Newport, with a new lodge and cemetery gates.

Looking across the cemetery, with the grave of historian Kathleen Major and her sister, Eileen, in the foreground. (*Andrew Walker*).

By this date, the cemetery accommodated many war graves in a section specifically dedicated to this purpose. It was located close to the 4th Northern General Hospital which had occupied the site of the Grammar School on Wragby Road during the First World War. A total of 1400 beds were available for the treatment of the war wounded and approximately 45,000 patients were accommodated there. Some 138 British, Canadian and Australian servicemen died in the hospital, and many were buried in Newport Cemetery. Of the 139 First World War burials in the cemetery today of British service personnel, the vast majority were of men who had died in the hospital. Ninety of them were buried together in a consolidated war graves plot. A few of those initially buried in Newport Cemetery were later exhumed and reinterred elsewhere, including ten American troops whose bodies were returned to the USA. The war graves section of the cemetery was expanded during and immediately after the Second World War when a further 120 burials took place.

The Cross of Sacrifice. (Andrew Walker).

During the First World War itself, a series of complaints were made about the care of the soldiers' graves at the cemetery, which one correspondent in the local paper described in June 1915 as 'neglected and forlorn'. These included criticisms from some of the patients themselves who were upset at the way in which their dead comrades were being treated. A theft of ribbons at the graveside of a recent war burial was also reported. In response to such negative comments, at a meeting of the City Council's Parks and Cemeteries Committee in July 1915, it was agreed that the graves of the war dead at the cemetery, amounting at that time to 22 such burials, would be turfed, maintained and wooden crosses added. A 'Committee of Ladies' was later set up who took responsibility for ensuring that fresh flowers were regularly placed on these soldier's graves, until November 1917, when it was reported that, to give the turf a rest, and the scarcity and cost of flowers, this practice ceased. By then, some 40 war dead were buried in the cemetery.

On Sunday 30 September 1923, a cross of sacrifice, erected by the Imperial War Graves Commission, was unveiled at the cemetery, memorialising the 144 First World War servicemen from Britain, Canada and Australia who were buried in the cemetery at that time. The memorial, made of Portland stone, was a replica of the cross of sacrifice, designed by Sir Reginald Blomfield and used extensively in many British war cemeteries including in France and Belgium. It stood 14 feet 6 inches in height, octagonal in shape, and with a stone base, which allowed room for the laying of wreaths. By the time of the memorial's unveiling, all of those interred in this section of the cemetery had uniformly sized Portland headstones on their graves, giving this part of Lincoln the feel of the much larger British war cemeteries overseas. At the ceremony, the City of Lincoln Council was also thanked for donating space within the municipal cemetery for the accommodation of the war dead.

The war graves plot, maintained by the Commonwealth War Graves Commission on land donated by City of Lincoln Council. (*Andrew Walker*).

In an unveiling ceremony held on 25 June 1952, a crusader's sword was added to the top of the cross of sacrifice in order to remember those who died in war service between 1939 and 1945. This was also the work of the War Graves Commission, now under its chief architect, Edward Maufe. Amongst the Second World War military personnel laid to rest in Newport Cemetery were four servicewomen – Vera Goulding, aged 25, who served in the Women's Royal Naval Service; Daphne Norman, an 'aircraftwoman', aged 18, a sparkplug tester at RAF Conningsby, who died of pneumonia; Mary Satchell, aged 30, of Queen Alexandra's Imperial Military Nursing Service; and Laura Mary Ward, aged 21, an 'aircraft woman, first class', who had been based at Coleby Grange, near Navenby and died of a blood disorder.

In addition to the British war dead in the cemetery, there were also 43 graves of German servicemen, 15 from the First World War and 28 from the 1939–45 conflict. Many of these men had died in nearby prisoner-of-war camps. However, the German War Grave Commission (GWGC) decided to concentrate many of the German war dead buried in British cemeteries on to a single site. The City Council's Parks, Markets and Cemeteries Committee approved the removal of these bodies in June 1961. The following year, the exhumation team recruited to undertake this hazardous and arduous work by administrative staff at the GWGC's temporary Maidenhead office, came to Lincolnshire and undertook this 'concentration' process, removing the bodies from Newport Cemetery, and smaller numbers from several other sites in the county, including from cemeteries at Bourne, Grimsby, Kirton Lindsey and Stamford. These servicemen were re-buried in the newly opened German military cemetery at Cannock Chase, Staffordshire which, by its consecration in 1969, accommodated the remains of some 5000 German and Austrian military personnel from the two world wars.

Some of the white wooden crosses marking the 28 German war graves of the Second World War. The bodies were later exhumed and moved to the German war cemetery at Cannock Chase, Staffordshire. *Lincolnshire Echo*, 17 August 1960. (*Source: Mirrorpix*).

At present, there are nearly 27,000 named graves in Newport Cemetery which, as the many fresh floral tributes demonstrate, remains an important site of mourning, remembrance and reflection.

Canwick Road 'Old' Cemetery

Arthur Ward

By the late 1840s it was becoming obvious that many of Lincoln's graveyards, under the control of the church, were full and provision hopelessly inadequate to accommodate further interments. Stories abounded of burials being no more than two feet underground in St Andrew's churchyard, dogs digging up mounds, the stench of the graveyards, and lads defacing tombstones.

A suitable site for a general cemetery had to be found, for which the consent of the bishop and all the parochial clergy, as well as all parties living nearby, would be required. The only graveyard still suitable for burials was the new St Swithin's cemetery, situated next to Rosemary Lane.

The Public Health Act of 1848 and a subsequent series of Burial Acts, notably those of 1850, 1852 and 1853, allowed for the closure of churchyards and the creation of burial boards. These burial boards and their associated new cemeteries were established by individual churches at St Nicholas and St John (Newport) and at St Peter in Eastgate and St Margaret (near to Langworthgate).

The procrastination of the city's other parishes meant that it was not until January 1855, seven years after the Public Health Act was made statute, that all the cemeteries were officially closed, except the St Swithin's cemetery on Rosemary Lane. Closures were ordered following an official visit from a member of the Central Board of Health in 1854. On 2 February 1855, it was reported in the *Lincolnshire Chronicle* that, with the exception of the parish of St Swithin's, all of the other parishes within the city which were not served by a burial board would combine together to form one for the whole number, comprising the parishes of St Benedict, St Botolph, St Peter-at-Arches, St Peter-at-Gowts, St Mark, St Mary-le-Wigford, St Martin, St Michael on the Mount, and St Paul.

One further issue had also arisen. The powers of the Nonconformist movement had been getting stronger and, by 1847, cemeteries could be divided into consecrated and unconsecrated parts. By 1852, division became obligatory, with consecrated ground being available principally for Anglicans and unconsecrated ground for Nonconformists. The issue of the cemetery would become a battleground between Chapel and Church.

Agreement was eventually reached by the burial board that they would purchase 15 acres of land from the Council adjoining Canwick Road, on ground that, at the time, still formed part of the South Common. The decision to develop the Canwick Road site as a cemetery was highly contentious: 42 votes were cast in its favour by burial board members but with

A view across the cemetery. (*Andrew Walker*).

23 votes, among them several loud voices, advancing the case for a cemetery to be laid out instead on the north-eastern part of the West Common. The critics of the majority view were to an extent quietened when Mr Grainger, the Government Inspector, appointed to approve the land chosen, indicated that the soil was of a very suitable quality on the Canwick Road site, but that the clay on the West Common would have deemed the location unfit for the development of a cemetery.

With the rise of the architectural profession following the granting of its royal charter in 1837, the upsurge of the economy in the Victorian era, and the increase in wealth and population, the control of development became paramount. Architects were being commissioned for projects and to seek competition for this work *The Builder* magazine (founded in 1843) became the vehicle for advertising them.

The establishment of the burial boards, following the Burial Acts of 1852, stimulated these boards to seek competitive designs for their town cemeteries. Between 1850 and 1860 some

88 competitions were announced in *The Builder,* Lincoln's being one of them, in 1855. Overall, some 162 were recorded nationally.

The editions of *The Builder* on 5 and 12 May 1855 included advertisements inviting entrants for a competition to design Lincoln's new cemetery. Two chapels were specified, one for Anglicans, the other for Nonconformists and a maximum amount of £500 was to be expended on each one. In the event, and after the competition had closed, in part as a response to criticisms of penny pinching, it was agreed that a total of £1500 could be spent on both, with equal amounts being allocated to each of the chapels. Amongst the complaints made was an editorial on 8 June 1855 in the *Lincolnshire Chronicle,* which declared that, with regard to the new cemetery, 'surely the capital of the county ought to set an example of taste to other places' so that it should be 'equal, at least in appearance, to any burial ground in the county.'

Although the prominent architect George Gilbert Scott was appointed as the competition's referee, owing to other work commitments he was unable to do so, and instead he recommended the appointment of John Loughborough Pearson to undertake the refereeing. Pearson had recently restored the chancel of Stow church.

Twenty-seven entries were received, and limited prize monies of £10 and £5 were to be awarded to the first two selected, although these were not necessarily the final choices to undertake the work. Pearson identified the best six entries for the chapels, lodge and 'dead house', and a further six plans relating to the layout of the cemetery, placing them in order of merit. The burial board finally selected the plans of Michael Drury for the buildings and Henry Goddard's design for the cemetery layout, losing its Vice Chairman, Rev. J.S. Gibney, along the way. He resigned when the application of 'Hope', Bellamy and Hardy's buildings design, was initially selected. Gibney declared that those who had voted for 'Hope' had done so to support a friend.

The competition proved a controversial one, with several of the applicants complaining about the result, noting that the referee's decisions were ignored in favour of Lincoln-based entries. Pearson's preferred buildings design, not selected by the burial board, was by the London-based architects Cooper & Peck – submitted as 'Justitia' – who, according to the *Stamford Mercury* on 17 August 1855 had written to the clerk of the burial board stating, using 'seasoned language', that 'they had never been treated by any paltry burial board in the country as the Lincoln Board had treated them'. *The Builder* had noted in its report of the competition on 30 June 1855 that 'Justitia' had provided information about 'other works being performed under their direction', thereby disclosing their identity, contrary to the conditions of the contest. Other applicants demanded compensation because their plans

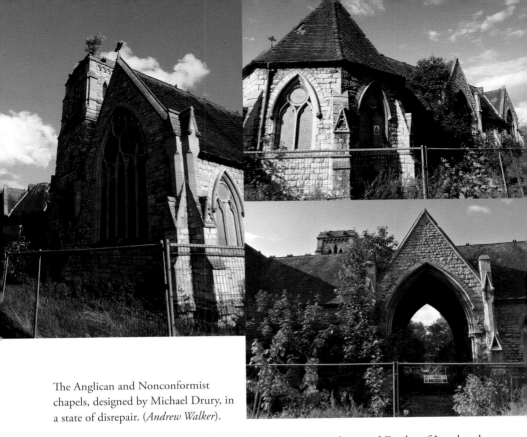

The Anglican and Nonconformist chapels, designed by Michael Drury, in a state of disrepair. (*Andrew Walker*).

had been returned to them in a damaged condition. Maugham and Fowler of Louth, whose submission for the cemetery layout had been particularly praised by the referee, had a letter to the *Lincolnshire Chronicle* printed in the issue of 27 July 1855, in which they expressed surprise that the selected entry of Henry Goddard had not even been mentioned by Pearson.

The likely expenditure on the cemetery is recorded in an article in *The Church Building News* of 18 August 1855 and comprised the following:

Chapel	£1500
Lodge and Dead House	£400
Drainage, Formation, Roads, Walls, Fence, Etc.	£2000
Architects' commission 5%	£175
Purchase of land	£1125
Vicar of Canwick: Right	£100
Hearses Etc.	£200
Law expenses and Premiums	£200
TOTAL:	£5700

A loan of £7000 from the General Annuity Endowment Association was obtained by the burial board to undertake the work. The majority of the building work and layout of the cemetery was undertaken, for the sum of £2200, by the Lincoln-based contractor William Huddlestone. By1870, he was serving on the burial board's finance committee.

On Friday 26 October 1855 the burial board met at the Guildhall from where a procession of some 2000 children walked to the Canwick Road site. It was noted in the *Lincolnshire Chronicle* that 'by the time some children reached the site walking along Canwick Road, others were still on Oxford Street'. Entrance to the ceremony was by ticket only. The first stone of the chapel was laid by Richard Carline, chairman of the burial board, using the same trowel as had been employed at a similar event at the Corn Exchange in 1847. The foundation stone contained a bottle within which had been placed coins of the realm, a roll of parchment inscribed with the names of members of the burial board, clerks and officials. A brass plate on the stone was also inscribed: 'The chapel was consecrated by the Bishop of Lincoln on 9th November 1855'. A further dedication stone was inscribed with the name of the architect, M. Drury. Consecration of the cemetery took place on 30 July 1856, with the Bishop of Lincoln conducting the ceremony.

By 14 March 1856, the *Stamford Mercury* was reporting favourably on the progress undertaken on the two new chapels in the cemetery grounds, which it described as of 'picturesque appearance' and 'are marked by rich design and skilled workmanship. When finished, with the addition of the tower and spire, they will prove creditable to the discrimination of the burial board and the genius of the architect (Mr. M. Drury), and will probably be adopted as models for other cemetery chapels.'

The design of the two chapels was in the Gothic Revival style, which was particularly fashionable in the mid-nineteenth century. The Anglican and Nonconformist chapels were linked by a lofty, arched open carriage-way. Although both chapels were designed in the same architectural manner, built of the same material and similar sums of money were spent on each, they were markedly different, as the *Stamford Mercury* noted on 1 August 1856, when detailed descriptions were given of each chapel. Of the Nonconformist building, the paper commented, it is:

> an octagonal structure, lighted by three handsome four-light windows: on the exterior, these windows have gables over them; in the interior, the woodwork or the gable roofs intersect those of the main octagonal roof with a happy effect; but the crowning feature of the chapel is the lantern, which is suspended in the

centre. This lantern is a component part of the roof, every main timber in it being necessary to a firm and scientific construction. The result is highly satisfactory: the rays of light streaming from its four small dormers rest upon and pick out the simple tracery and carved bosses distributed amongst the interlacing timbers, giving that varying light and shade which is so pleasing.

The Anglican chapel was described as follows:

> Perhaps the most striking feature of the front is the large end window … Although this front be most prominent, yet the other [windows] have been completed with the same care and finish, showing an evident wish to make all points of view equally satisfactory … [The] ecclesiastical chapel, which is built in the conventional form of church, is adapted to its peculiar requirements.

Particular emphasis was placed in the report upon the Anglican chapel's 'very handsome chancel arch' and its tower with staircase, placed 'to give access to the belfry', ensuring that it was taller than its Nonconformist counterpart.

Of the design and layout of the cemetery, this was clearly recorded on J.S. Padley's map of 1868, with an entrance shown off Pelham Street (now Canwick Road). The adjacent lodge was designed in a similar architectural style to the chapels to the south, next to Washingborough Road. The 'Dead House' was shown adjacent to the northern boundary. Later alterations saw the main

Grave of Michael Drury, architect of the Canwick Road Cemetery chapels. (*Michael J. Jones*).

vehicular entrance moved from Canwick Road to Washingborough Road at the south-east end of the site.

Today this cemetery, opened for burials in 1856, and in which to date 31,812 named individuals have been buried, is administered by the City of Lincoln Council; the lodge (with outbuildings) is still occupied, and the mortuary is retained as a store. However, despite attempts to secure a new use, the condition of the Grade II-listed chapel buildings continue to deteriorate.

The Burial Boards, St Swithin's Cemetery, Washingborough Road and Canwick Road 'New' Cemetery

Andrew Walker

St Swithin's Cemetery on Washingborough Road and Canwick Road 'New' Cemetery are respectively the second and third oldest constituent elements of the funerary complex to the south east of Lincoln's city centre, the oldest part of which is the cemetery considered in Arthur Ward's previous chapter, and the newest element is the crematorium, which is examined in a subsequent chapter.

St Swithin's Cemetery

The parish of St Swithin declined to join with nine other, mainly 'below hill' parishes, to form the Lincoln Burial Board which opened in 1856 and maintained the Canwick Road cemetery. This was because, at the time of the burial board's institution, St Swithin's had very recently developed its own new cemetery, on an acre of land immediately to the east of Rosemary Lane. However, with the rapid growth of St Swithin's parish, the city's largest, the new cemetery quickly filled and the parish undertook increasingly urgent measures to find more suitable burial spaces for its parishioners.

The St Swithin's Burial Board, formally founded in October 1877, comprising the vicar, four Anglicans and four Nonconformists, negotiated with the Lincoln Burial Board responsible for the Canwick Road cemetery and came to an arrangement whereby, for the sum of £40 a year, St Swithin's parishioners could be buried in the Canwick Road cemetery. The St Swithin's Burial Board had been set up largely owing to concerns about the need to find alternative burial accommodation for its parishioners as the Rosemary Lane site was becoming filled. At its first meeting, the Board decided that, rather than acquiring land for a new cemetery, it would be more economical and convenient to make use of the general cemetery on Canwick Road. However, by the 1880s, the Canwick Road 15-acre site was itself becoming increasingly congested and the Lincoln Burial Board, too, was beginning to seek additional grounds. Some attempts were made to unite the two burial boards but this proved unsuccessful, with harsh words exchanged on both sides.

In 1883, the Canwick Road Burial Board sought to continue to impose the increased annual fee charged to the St Swithin's board of £50. The St Swithin's board attempted to reduce this to the original £40. As the *Stamford Mercury* reported on 11 May 1883, in its account of a recent meeting of the Lincoln Burial Board: 'After consideration this was declined, and it was ordered that St Swithin's Burial Board have the right of burial in the Canwick-road burial ground upon the same terms as last year for another year ending 14th August, 1884,

St Swithin Burial Board's first cemetery on Rosemary Lane. (*Andrew Walker*).

and unless they are prepared to contribute accordingly they be requested to make other arrangements for the burial of their dead.'

Some members of the Lincoln Burial Board were opposed to the St Swithin's parish continuing to make use of the Canwick Road cemetery. Several on the Board felt that St Swithin's was not paying its way, compared to member parishes of the Lincoln Board, which had between them paid £7000 for the land and £3600 in interest, excluding the annual maintenance costs; others, such as Mr J.H. Folley, speaking in May 1878, thought that St Swithin's, by far the largest parish in the city, accommodating nearly one-fifth of its population in 1881, 'would soon fill the cemetery'.

Later that year, the ongoing negotiations between St Swithin's Burial Board and the Lincoln Burial Board broke down further, leading to the following resolution being passed at a Lincoln Burial Board meeting in November 1883: 'That no person who has died in the parish of St. Swithin, in the city of Lincoln, be buried in the burial-ground next to the

Memorial chapel at St Swithin's cemetery, Washingborough Road. (*Andrew Walker*).

Canwick Road after the 31st December, 1884.' By this date, in this cemetery, some 60 to 70 interments a year were from St Swithin's.

Dr Hoffman, one of the Government Inspectors in the Burials Department in the Home Office, observed at a meeting in August 1885, with some understatement, that 'there was a little friction between the two Boards'. Animosity seemed particularly intense between Rev. G.H. Pratt of St Swithin's and the long-serving clerk to the Lincoln Burial Board, Thurstan Dale. Hoffman had inspected the St Swithin's cemetery and declared it full. He noted that the Lincoln Burial Board was acting reasonably and had given the St Swithin's Burial Board ample time to find land for its own cemetery. Dale claimed that the Lincoln Board, sometimes referred to from 1885 onwards as the Canwick Road Burial Board, would be within its rights to lock the cemetery gates to prevent burials from St Swithin's but realised that it would be impossible to do so.

Further threats were made by the Lincoln Burial Board: it was stated that no further St Swithin's burials would be allowed after 31 December 1889. Finally, a resolution to the difficulty arose when suitable land was provided for the St Swithin's Burial Board. As reported in the *Stamford Mercury* on 6 September 1889, Mr C. C. Sibthorp who owned extensive lands in Canwick, agreed to offer for sale to the St Swithin's Burial Board six acres of land adjoining Washingborough Road. At a meeting of parishioners in the newly built St Swithin's vestry room in Free School Lane in September 1889, it was agreed to proceed with the purchase of the land at a competitive price of £1500 and to construct a chapel, erect fences and lay out the grounds for a further £2000. Although the sale was only formally finalised in 1890, the foundation stone of the St Swithin's cemetery chapel bears the year 1889, which perhaps is indicative of the burial board's eagerness to ensure the cemetery was opened promptly following the securing of the land. Part of the new burial ground was consecrated on 8 March 1890 by the Bishop of Lincoln, Edward King.

Canwick Road 'new' cemetery

C.C. Sibthorp also provided land – at a price – to enable an extension to be made to the Canwick Road Cemetery. The 'New Cemetery' was developed on land close to the cemetery of 1856, but not immediately adjoining it. Several members of the burial board challenged the use of the term 'extension' since the additional burial ground was not connected to the old cemetery. The *Lincolnshire Chronicle*, on 15 May 1896, noted that the present 14-acre cemetery accommodated a total of 10,568 grave spaces – composed of 1390 first-class, 3220 second-class, and 5958 third-class. The new ground was smaller, just over ten acres, and if the plans recommended were adopted, it would provide grave spaces for 1422 first-class, 2707 second-class, and 6201 third-class, with 60 grave spaces reserved, making a total of 10,390 – 178 fewer graves than the 'old' cemetery on nearly four acres less of land.

First-class grave sites, unsurprisingly, occupied the most prestigious parts of the cemetery, located close to the main walks and offering the best panoramic views. In addition to the cost of the grave site, various charges were made for the furnishing of the grave itself. The Canwick Road Burial Board price list is detailed below, as it stood in February 1886:

'Headstones without bases, 5 shillings (s); with bases not exceeding 12 inches in width and height, 7s.6d.; with bases exceeding 12 inches and not exceeding 15 inches in width and height, 10s.; kerbstones, 5s.; monumental crosses not exceeding 5 feet is height, on oblong bases, 10s.; all other monuments, tombs, or stones, £1.'

In the case of third-class graves, which were more tightly packed together, the Lincoln Burial Board did not allow headstones to be erected, as was noted in the *Lincolnshire Chronicle* on 12 August 1892.

Looking across St Swithin's cemetery towards the chapel. (*Andrew Walker*).

The economies in the new cemetery extended to the fact that no chapel was constructed. Instead, for those to be interred in the new cemetery, services could be conducted in the existing cemetery chapels on the Canwick Road site. At the opening of the new cemetery, when reports mentioned the recently built commodious new lodge and mortuary which were part of the development, it was noted that a road or path directly connecting the two cemeteries would be constructed in due course.

The lack of ready internal access between the two cemeteries prompted some criticism and it was observed that, following the reception of the coffin at the cemetery chapel, it then had to be conveyed 150 to 200 yards along a public road to the new cemetery for the interment. By 1900, complaints continued to be made, particularly by clergy, about the arrangements, including the new road linking the two cemeteries. In its account of a burial board meeting, the *Lincolnshire Echo* reported on 14 February 1900 that the Rev. Edmund Akenhead, vicar of St Martin, 'wished the Canwick Road Burial Board would see to the road (if you could call it one) to the new cemetery, as it was very bad for them to walk down, when a body was to be buried in that part. He also asked if a chapel could be built in the new cemetery. It was very inconvenient for them to go to the old one, and then have to carry the coffins a long way to get to the new cemetery.'

Some years before the Canwick Road New Cemetery was opened, in 1887 the burial board gave consideration to the proportions of any new cemetery site that should be set aside for consecrated and unconsecrated lands. Many Nonconformists and Roman Catholics opted to be buried on land unconsecrated by the Anglican clergy. It was reported at the burial board meeting that, recently, three-fifths of burials were on consecrated land and two-fifths on unconsecrated land. Consequently, it was agreed to apply such a division with any additional land secured and it was agreed that there should be a specific section for Roman Catholic burials.

Later the same year, the burial board was informed that some Nonconformists preferred to be buried in consecrated land alongside other family members who were Anglicans. Nonconformist ministers were prepared to conduct services on consecrated land, having gained the necessary permission of Anglican clergy in whose parish the deceased had resided. This had been made possible only recently, with the passing of the 1880 Burial Laws Amendment Act, against much Anglican opposition, including from the Bishop of Lincoln, Christopher Wordsworth. A certain reluctance to engage with the spirit of this new law can be discerned from the fact that payment for the service for Nonconformist burials in consecrated ground had to be made to the Anglican clergy concerned, even though it was a Nonconformist minister undertaking the ceremony, who received no payment.

With Lincoln's ongoing expansion and the proliferation of parochial bodies required to administer it, the city council, in common with other urban authorities, sought to rationalise its governance. Following Lincoln City Council's representations to the Local Government Board, and despite opposition by the city's burial boards and the Board of Guardians, it was agreed by the Local Government Board that the city should become a unified parish for many administrative purposes. This unification scheme came into effect on 31 March 1907 which meant, from that date, that a single Cemeteries Department was instituted at the city's Corporation Offices, that equal rights of burial applied across the city, and the separate, often disputatious, separate burial boards – namely the Lincoln Burial Board and the burial boards of the parishes of St Swithin, St Nicholas with St John, and St Peter in Eastgate with St Margaret – ceased to exist. Rather immodestly, the Chairman of the Lincoln Burial Board, Thomas Jackson, at its meeting in November 1906, expressed the hope that the Corporation would keep the cemetery in the same state of perfection as they found it.

LINCOLN`S NINETEENTH-CENTURY CAMPAIGN VETERANS REMEMBERED

Paul Hickman

No matter how valiantly servicemen fought in the great campaigns of the early and mid-nineteenth century, it is usually only the officers who were commemorated by grand churchyard memorials and glowing obituaries. Some of Lincoln`s 'sons' who fought in the Peninsular campaign and at Waterloo, the Afghan War, the Crimean War, and the Indian Mutiny, and who are buried in Lincoln`s churchyards and cemeteries, are thus remembered.

Lincoln-born Major Charles Lowrie served in the 69th Grenadier (South Lincolnshire) Regiment of Foot (1793–1814). He was appointed an ensign in 1802, and promoted to Lieutenant in 1804. Lowrie was present at the capture of Java in 1811, and in the successful attack on Redoubt No. 2 at Fort Cornelis on 26 August of the same year, where he was severely wounded by being shot through the body. Lowrie was promoted to Captain in June 1812, and was advanced to Major, by purchase, on 28 August 1826, and exchanged to the Unattached List on half-pay in November 1828. He was retrospectively awarded the Java campaign clasp to his general military medal in 1847. Major Lowrie died at Lincoln on the 18th November 1855, aged 70, and was buried in St. Mark`s churchyard, which has since been redeveloped, after partial excavation in 1976.

Another native of Lincoln, Sir Richard Armstrong, was the only son of Lt.-Col. Richard Armstrong. He was commissioned as an ensign in 1796, and served in the Peninsular War from 1808 to the end of the campaign in 1814, reaching the rank of Lieutenant-Colonel. Armstrong saw service in many battle areas, and, while commanding Portuguese regiments in the Pyrenees in 1813, was severely wounded in the arm. He continued in the service of Portugal for six years after the conclusion of the Napoleonic Wars. For his distinguished war record Richard was given the freedom of the city of Lincoln in 1821.

Armstrong then served as a Brigadier in the first Burmese War, in the campaigns of 1825–26. He stormed and carried the stockades near Prome in December 1825. Armstrong was promoted to the rank of Colonel in 1830 and knighted a year later for his military service. He became commander of the British forces in Canada West between 1842 and 1848. In 1849 Armstrong was gazetted Colonel of the 95th Foot, and a year later he became colonel of the 32nd Foot. Following his appointment as Commander-in-Chief of the Madras presidency in 1851, that November he was promoted to Lieutenant-General. A Knight Commander of the Portuguese orders of St. Benedict of Avis and of the Tower and Sword, Armstrong was made a Knight Commander of the Bath (KCB) in 1852. His continued ill health forced him to resign his command in Madras in early 1854. Armstrong died off the island of St.

Helena on his homeward voyage on board the *Barham* on March 3rd 1854, at the age of 72, and was buried at sea. There is a memorial window to him in Lincoln Cathedral. This depicts Bible scenes (passages in the life of David) and the family shield, with the distinctions of knighthood and the family quarterings of the deceased, and the representation of 12 different orders conferred upon him.

Captain Francis Kennedy died on 4 May 1857, aged 69, at his home in the Bail, and was buried in Eastgate cemetery. This highly decorated Peninsular and Waterloo veteran was first gazetted ensign in the 51st Regiment of Light Infantry in 1809, becoming Lieutenant two years later. Francis went through the whole campaign (1809–15). He was at the siege and capture of Flushing, both sieges of Badajoz, and that at Ciudad Rodrigo, and was present at the retreat from Burgos.

Francis also saw action at Val Moresco, Peyrehorade and Echalar, and fought in the battles of Fuentes d'Onoro, Salamanca, Vitoria, Pampeluna, Pyrenees, Nive, Orthes and Waterloo. He also led the column of attack at the storming of Combray. Francis later became Adjutant and Captain of the North Lincoln Militia in 1824 until his retirement in 1853.

Also buried in Eastgate cemetery was Lincoln-born Captain John Willson R.N. In 1797 he was apprenticed to the merchant service. In 1803 he was impressed into the navy, and saw action on board several ships, off Fecamp, Boulogne and the Bay of Algeciras. Between 1806 and 1810, John served with the *Milan* off the coast of North America and the West Indies. Returning to Europe he was involved in the capture of several French vessels as he worked his way through the ranks, becoming a First Lieutenant in 1815. Willson obtained his commission as Commander in 1841, retiring on half pay a year later. He died at his Lindum Road residence on 4 December 1864, aged 82.

In St. Helen's churchyard, Boultham, lies an unusual war memorial. It is a large granite stone block brought back from the walls of Sebastopol by Major Richard G. Ellison, in

Tomb of Captain Francis Kennedy in Eastgate Cemetery. (*Paul Hickman*).

A granite stone block in St Helen's churchyard, Boultham, in memory of men serving under Major Richard G. Ellison who had died during the Crimean War. (*Paul Hickman*).

memory of his men who had died during the Crimean War. On the right of the block is a round depression with small cracks radiating from it, typical of a strike by a shell. In front are two mortar shells, slightly set into the ground.

Sir Richard Ellison C.V.O., D.L. died suddenly on 27 February 1908 at Brighton, aged 77. Born in 1831 at Boultham, son of Colonel Richard Ellison, Richard (junior) served with distinction and valour in the Crimean campaign (1854–55) with the 47th Lancashire Foot Regiment. Ellison was present at the Battles of Alma and Inkerman, and the capture of Balaclava, and served through the siege of Sebastopol. During one of his engagements Ellison had a narrow escape when a bullet passed through the cap he was wearing. Ellison retired from the army with the rank of Major. Later, he served for 35 years with the 2nd Volunteer Battalion Lincolnshire Regiment, a great part of the time as Commander.

From 1861, Ellison became a Justice of the Peace, remaining so until his death. In 1886 he was elected High Sheriff of the county. He became Deputy-Lieutenant of Lincolnshire (D.L.), and a Commander of the Royal Victorian Order (C.V.O.) in 1902. Knighted in 1907, he was the oldest member of the King's Yeoman of the Guard. A measure of the esteem in which he was held can be gauged by the large concourse of people who witnessed the funeral cortege, as it made its way to St. Helen's churchyard.

Local newspapers did occasionally report on the deaths of ordinary veteran soldiers. John Healey enlisted with the 17th Regiment of Foot, in Leicester, in 1832. He was stationed in

Australia near to a penal colony, then on the outbreak of the Afghan War in 1839 the regiment proceeded to Afghanistan where John took part in several severe engagements. These included the storming and capture of Ghazni, and the battle of Khelat. The 17th then served in India for about ten years, followed by garrison duty at Aden. It was from here that John was invalided home, having suffered severely from dysentery. He was discharged from the army in 1853, after 21 years' service (11 as Corporal). John had been born near Rugby but on retiring from the army he came to live in Lincoln to be near his son. Here, John joined the permanent staff of the Royal North Lincoln Militia, becoming a Staff Sergeant, eventually retiring into private life in 1871. He died on 1 April 1896 at his son's house, at 37 Boultham Road, aged 88, and was buried in Canwick Road Old Cemetery.

The Ellison memorial in St. Helen's churchyard. (*Paul Hickman*).

Ex-Sergeant James Blackburn, of Avondale Street, Lincoln, died on 11 May 1909, aged 74, and was buried in St. Swithin's cemetery. He enlisted in the Royal North Lincoln Militia in 1854, and volunteered the following year for active service in the Crimea with the 38th Foot Regiment. Following this campaign his regiment was in the thick of the fighting in the 1857 Indian Rebellion. After forced marches to Cawnpore, the 38th were engaged in the defeat of the Gwalior contingent, and formed part of the pursuing columns. Sergeant Blackburn was at the relief of Lucknow, and formed one of the party storming the Kaiserbagh. He left the army invalided in 1874.

In 1902 and 1903, to generate some extra income, he appeared in the local press talking about his miraculous cure after 40 years of suffering with terrible kidney trouble caused by the hardships of his army service. Doctors had told him it was quite useless to give him medicine. 'But it isn't in a British soldier to give up hope, and I struggled on', he said. Blackburn was promoting Dean's Backache Kidney Pills, which could be bought from Boot's High Street store at 2s. 9d. a box, or 13s. 9d. for six boxes. After a full course he exclaimed, 'They positively cured me a year ago, and ever since that time I have not had the slightest backache or rheumatism'.

Remembering Lincoln's Civilian War Dead (1939–45): Memorials and Graves

Hazel Kent

The Roll of Honour for civilians killed during the Second World War includes 19 individuals whose deaths occurred in Lincoln. Compiled by the Imperial War Graves Commission (IWGC) – later, in 1960, renamed the Commonwealth War Graves Commission – the Civilian War Dead Roll gathered information from the Registrar-General and local authorities. Those eligible for inclusion had died as a direct result of enemy action, or had been killed because of Allied military accidents, or had died at their post while undertaking Civil Defence duties. The 66,375 names were bound into seven volumes and presented in 1956 to Westminster Abbey.

The 19 fatalities for the 'County Borough of Lincoln' were recorded as: Harry Brown (aged 54 years), Beatrice Cook (47), Edith Fowle (49), Edith Gibbons (32), Eva Hall (20), Albert Liens (68), Margaret Marriott (12), Nellie Mastin (58), Alfred Medd (71), Harold Onn (34), Ernest Radford (59), Mary Rodgers (66), Elizabeth Spray (65), Anthony Thacker (three), Lena Thacker (38), Andrew Tollerton (27), Elsie Tollerton (two), Annie Whitby (42) and Lawrence Whitby (three).

Lincoln's own War Memorial Committee members also hoped to remember formally civilian casualties. At a meeting held on 20 September 1950, they decided: 'Civilian air raid casualties [should] be included in a separate panel on the War Memorial and on a separate page in the Memory Book.' However, progress on the broader question of an appropriate memorial for the city's fallen had already been much delayed following an initial meeting in July 1946. The difficulty of agreeing to the form that a memorial should take, and raising sufficient funds, meant that final arrangements were not proceeded with until the mid-1950s, as is examined in the chapter by Arthur Ward and Andrew Walker.

An ambitious proposal to establish a housing scheme for disabled veterans was scrapped, and, in the end, a decision was taken to add the names of fallen Armed Services personnel and civilian casualties to the existing First World War memorial at St. Benedict's on the High Street and to the Memory Book held at the Central Library. In addition, the churchyard to the rear of St. Benedict's was to be transformed into a Garden of Remembrance.

Members of the local War Memorial Committee do not appear to have had access to the same information as the IWGC; instead, they compiled a list of names by asking the public

Lincoln City war memorial, St. Benedict's Square. The panel incorporating civilians' names sits to the left of the central panel at the front of the monument. (*All photographs by Hazel Kent*).

to provide details of eligible relatives. Criteria for eligibility appear somewhat ambiguous: in 1946 Committee minutes stated that servicemen had to live in Lincoln at the outbreak of war to qualify, whereas later reports stated that they had to live in the city at the time of enlistment. No evidence has been located of criteria for civilian inclusion or any discussion of this. It seems most likely that, in common with the IWGC's approach, deaths which occurred within Lincoln were eligible, although it is possible that residence in the city at the start of the war was a further requirement.

Understandably, newspaper appeals for names focused on the Armed Forces. Some articles briefly mentioned that civilians were to be included, whilst others omitted this information entirely. It can therefore be suggested that most relatives of civilian casualties were simply unaware of the intention to include them. As a result, when the new memorial tablets for the Second World War were unveiled by Lincoln's Mayor on the misty, wet morning of 6 November 1955, only four civilians were honoured. The *Lincolnshire Echo's* report on the dedication service, led by the Bishop of Grimsby, made no mention of civilians. On the tablets they, like the service personnel, were identified only by surname and initials: Brown, H., Marriott, M., Onn, H., and Radford, E.A. Despite the Committee's original intentions, civilians did not have their own panel, but were listed separately after the Armed Forces casualties. This was also the case in the Memory Book, completed in 1958, with the same four individuals listed on the final page with scant detail.

The youngest person named on Lincoln's war memorial in St Benedict's Square is Margaret Marriott, only 12 years old when a Lancaster bomber, on a training flight from RAF Wigsley, crashed and destroyed her home at 25 Highfield Avenue. Margaret was at home alone, completing homework, when the devastating incident occurred on 11 June 1943. She died of suffocation and burns. Her parents, Basil and Hilda Marriott, had gone to their allotment and ran home after seeing the crash, to find their house on fire. Margaret was laid to rest in St. Helen's Churchyard, Boultham.

In October 1955, just three weeks before the unveiling of the Second World War tablets on Lincoln's war memorial, Hilda Marriott wrote to the Secretary of the War Memorial Committee, G.E. Smalley. In a moving letter that survives in the Lincolnshire Archives, Mrs Marriott asks if her daughter's name is included, explaining: 'Her name has not been submitted by me, as I did not know – until I read the *Chronicle* today – that civilians were to be included. Also, I do not know if her death would be termed a war casualty.' Mr Smalley acted swiftly, telephoning the architect at Watkins, Coombes and Partners confirming instructions to add Margaret's name to the memorial. Hilda Marriott wrote to thank him: 'Margaret was very dear to our hearts, & altho [sic] we ourselves will never forget her, it will be nice to feel her name will always be remembered'.

Of the other three civilian names included on the city's war memorial, there was another victim of an RAF accident. Ernest Radford died on 27 July 1941 when two planes collided in mid-air and crashed onto Oxford Street. Mr Radford, who lived at 46 Shakespeare Street, was a passer-by in a car which was hit by part of the plane and 'torn to ribbons' by the explosion. He had worked as a Director at Messrs Gilberts which sold 'Cycles and Accessories' and had

Margaret Marriott's grave: 'Treasured Memories of our dearly loved daughter, Margaret Elaine Marriott. Taken suddenly 11th June 1943, Aged 12 Years. There's a friend for little children.' The statuette was originally an angel; the wings have now been lost. (*Hazel Kent*).

premises on Oxford Street. Mr Radford was also a firewatcher. He was buried at Canwick Road New Cemetery, Plot K112.

Harry Brown and Harold Onn, the other civilians named on the war memorial, were both killed as a result of a significant German air raid on the night of 15 January 1943. Mr Brown was an Air Raid Warden on duty when he was killed by a bomb striking the air-raid shelter near his home in Avondale Street. He was buried at Canwick Road New Cemetery, Plot D971. Harold Onn, of 5 Mill Row, died in the early hours of the morning following the raid when a delayed action firebomb exploded on Bank Street, damaging the gas-main he was inspecting. The father of three was interred at St. Paul's Church in Grimsby.

The remaining 15 civilian casualties for Lincoln, named on the IWGC's Roll of Honour, are missing from the war memorial at St. Benedict's. Several of these individuals died in the same incidents as those named on the tablet. Lena Thacker, Annie Whitby and their two young sons, Anthony and Lawrence all died as a result of the Highfield Avenue Lancaster crash. They were buried together in St. Helen's churchyard, Boultham. Nellie Mastin and Elizabeth Spray lived next-door to each other in Oxford Street, and both died as a consequence of the same RAF accident that killed Ernest Radford. Elizabeth was killed instantly, whilst Nellie died later in the County Hospital after suffering terrible burns that left her blind. Elizabeth was buried in Canwick Road New Cemetery Plot T239, with Nellie in the nearby Old Cemetery, Plot A1713. Beatrice Cook was the third civilian who died in the large air raid on 15th January 1943. A cook in an RAF NAAFI, she was killed when the bus she was travelling on was hit by an incendiary bomb in St. Mary's Street. She was buried in All Saints churchyard, Wragby.

Andrew Tollerton and his young daughter Elsie were killed by an enemy air raid on 9 May 1941 at their home, 26 Westwick Drive. They were buried together at Canwick Road Old Cemetery, Plot A1712. Mary Rodgers was killed nearby in the same raid, at her bungalow, 4 Prial Close. Mrs Rodgers, a widow, was also buried at Canwick Road Old Cemetery, Plot 2758. On the same night, Waddington village was struck by German bombers. Eva Hall, of Barr Lane, Waddington, died of her injuries after being taken to Lincoln County Hospital. Her funeral took place in the Methodist Church, Waddington and she is listed on the war memorial plaque at St. Michael's Church, Waddington.

Edith Fowle, a French teacher at Lincoln Girls' High School, died on 22 July 1941 when a Hampden bomber crashed into the staff boarding house on Greestone Stairs. Miss Fowle was buried in Eastgate Cemetery, plot A401, and is remembered in Lincoln Christ Hospital's school memorial and Garton Archive. A former pupil at the Girls' High School, Edith Joyce Gibbons, was killed by enemy bombing on 13 August 1941 near her home at Newark Road, Swallowbeck. An ARP Ambulance driver, she was on fire-watching duty at the time. Albert Liens was also killed on fire-guard duty when the Plaza Cinema went up in flames on 24 May 1943. Contrary to some later reports, this fire was not caused by enemy action, but, as he was undertaking Civil Defence work at the time, his death is recorded on the Roll of Honour. He was laid to rest in Newport Cemetery. Alfred Medd, a veteran of the Boer and First World Wars and, at 71, the oldest of Lincoln's civilian casualties, died of injuries caused by enemy bombing on 24 March 1941. His grave is in Canwick Road New Cemetery, plot A1711.

Memorials to the Fallen in Eastgate Cemetery: A Survey of the Different Ways Soldiers, Sailors and Airmen are Commemorated in a Small Urban Cemetery

Andrew Priestley

Eastgate Cemetery, otherwise known as St Peter's Cemetery, is a small cemetery situated a mere half mile away from Lincoln Cathedral up a small private drive that runs alongside the Eastgate Tennis, Bowls, and Squash Club. As the name implies, the cemetery is linked to the nearby Church of St Peter-in-Eastgate, although it is a distance from the church grounds. Despite existing for over 100 years, with some of the older graves on the site dating back to the mid-to-late nineteenth century, Eastgate Cemetery remains relatively unknown. However, even as small and out of the way as it is, there are a plethora of military graves. The Commonwealth War Graves Commission (CWGC) has a website entry for Eastgate Cemetery, despite it not being a site officially managed by the Commission. This entry counts six known casualties and lists the names of five soldiers, with ranks ranging from Private to Company Serjeant Major. This website entry fails to tell the whole story of the military graves at Eastgate Cemetery, so this chapter is a site survey of military graves in a small civilian cemetery.

Within the cemetery, 12 military graves were found as part of this research, two of which have standard CWGC headstones, though one, for J. S. Bell, who died in 1940, is within a private plot demarked by a low kerb stone. The rest of the military dead are mainly commemorated on family memorials with an almost even spread between open and private plots. However, there are a few notable examples of graves that seem unusual. The first example is a grave for a Captain D. F. Miller, buried in 1975 at age 52, that looks similar to those issued by the CWGC, but with a slightly different shaped top and standing above a low stone marker dedicated to his widow, Barbara, who passed away in 2008. This is unusual, given that he was not in active combat at the time of his death, and so was not eligible for a CWGC headstone. Upon further research, his newspaper obituary reveals that he died at a Royal Air Force hospital with his family requesting that any money that otherwise would be spent buying flowers should instead be donated to the RAF Benevolent Fund. His ties to the Royal Air Force are probably why his family had a gravestone commissioned that superficially resembled a standard CWGC headstone as an act of respect for him and those that served alongside him, though when his wife passed away it must have been reset on top of her marker.

Another example of the variety of graves on the site is that of Private J. W. Naylor, a soldier who died on 13 October 1915. His name appears on the side of a grave seemingly erected

The gravestone of Flying Officer J. S. Bell. (*Andrew Priestley*).

primarily to the memory of his aunt or uncle. This is unusual as most family graves pertain to immediate family such as parents, direct descendants, and siblings. A potential reason as to why he is on a family grave not his own is that he was initially reported as missing in action rather than killed in action, disqualifying him from a CWGC headstone. While this is uncommon, it is not unheard of – although, in many of these cases, casualties would often remain on larger war memorials rather than being added to a pre-existing family grave. Unusually, he seems to be on both types, with his name also appearing on numerous memorials from the Loos memorial in Pas de Calais to the Middlesborough Cenotaph in Yorkshire. The Eastgate commemoration does appear on the Imperial War Museum's War Memorials Register, but the inscription records at the Lincoln Central Library note the memorial but oddly without including a reference to his name.

Ultimately what cases such as J. W. Naylor show is how important it is to use a broad base of resources when carrying out a survey of military graves within a cemetery. The best resource to start with is almost always the online database of the CWGC, as it often has most of the details of the military graves at a site including service numbers and burial records. However,

The gravestones of Captain D. F. Miller and his wife, Barbara. (*Andrew Priestley*).

as this survey has shown, that resource is not infallible. As some of the examples within Eastgate show, there are cases in which the CWGC database falls short for reasons that vary from those we would expect, such as deaths outside of combat to military personnel who died prior to the establishment of the Commission. Some others are inexplicable. The CWGC website states that there are six CWGC graves at Eastgate yet it only lists five and there are some who were clearly eligible for a CWGC headstone or at least being mentioned on their website who do not feature at all. For example, two men who died in 1917, Lieutenant William Anthony Taylor, who was killed in action near Ypres in 1917, and Lance Corporal Mark Parker, who died of his wounds at Etaples, are not recorded at Eastgate (although Taylor is recorded on the Menin Gate in Ypres according to the CWGC website).

Ultimately, with a site like Eastgate, it is best to use these resources to see what has already been established by prior surveys and investigations, then go to the site in person to confirm these findings and see if there are any other graves that the CWGC may have missed. A survey such as this clearly shows there are a variety of ways that people who have died in the Forces have been commemorated. What it cannot tell us is why different types of memorials were chosen, why some families merely added their name to a pre-existing family memorial, why some added a CWGC headstone to a pre-existing family plot and some made do with a standard headstone, but had the body placed in a small local cemetery rather than in a larger CWGC site like Newport Cemetery.

Entrance to Eastgate Cemetery. (*Andrew Walker*).

Andrew Priestley produced this chapter whilst a student on Bishop Grosseteste University's BA (Hons) Military History degree programme.

Lincoln's Emergency Mortuary during the Second World War

Derwin Gregory

Prior to Britain's declaration of war on Germany on 3 September 1939, the government had spent years preparing for mass destruction in the case of total war. The focus of the planning during the 1930s was the potential impact of aerial bombardment, and the anticipated high number of civilian casualties. Civil defence planning in the lead up to the Second World War was based on Britain's experience of aerial bombardment during the First World War, and observations of the important role aircraft had played in the Spanish Civil War. At the start of the Second World War, it was estimated, by using air raid casualty figures from Barcelona during the Spanish Civil War, that London could suffer 200,000 casualties during the first night of bombing alone. Beyond the capital, local authorities were also concerned by the potential number of deaths that would occur from aerial bombardment, such as the Portsmouth Medical Officer of Health who anticipated that each day of air raids could result in 500–550 deaths.

In January 1939, it was decided that, in the event of war, the management of the deaths resulting from aerial bombardment would fall under the responsibility of organisations which dealt with general casualties. During this month, responsibility for the dead transferred from the Home Office to the Ministry of Health. On 28 February 1939, the Ministry of Health sent Circular 1779 to all town clerks setting out the principles of emergency burial procedures. This circular notified the town clerks that the local authorities would be responsible for dealing with the war dead.

At a meeting of the City of Lincoln's Air Raid Precautions Committee which was held on 28 March 1939, Lincoln's town clerk reported receipt of Circular 1779, and the committee resolved to: review existing mortuary accommodation, and explore other buildings which could be used to supplement the city's provision; review existing and potential burial accommodation; review transport facilities for the movement of bodies; and to provisionally select a Mortuary Superintendent, who could become familiar with the duties connected to disposing of bodies due to war operations. Following the review of mortuary accommodation, the town clerk reported at the Air Raid Precautions Committee on 20 November 1939 that the Minister of Health had sanctioned the conversion of the West Common racecourse grandstand into an emergency mortuary at the estimated cost of £280.

The plans for the adaptation of the racecourse stand for mortuary purposes had been produced on 6 October 1939, and clearly show that it was proposed to segregate the building into areas for the living and the dead. Entrance to the morgue for grieving relatives, or those

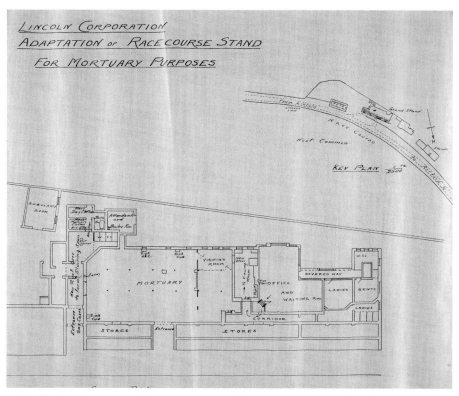

A plan for the adaptation of the racecourse stand for mortuary purposes by Alec Adlington, city engineer and surveyor, 6 October 1939. (*Source: Lincolnshire Archives, Lincoln City/ Eng/2/6/4/9*).

trying to locate the bodies of loved ones, was located at the rear of the building. On entering, one had immediate access to toilet facilities which provided an opportunity for the visitors to gather their composure before entering the light and airy office and waiting room. When the mortuary staff were ready, the visitor to the morgue would walk through a series of corridors and liminal spaces, before entering the viewing room which was accessed via a new doorway that had been knocked through the structure. The viewing room was screened from the rest of the mortuary, which provided a 'sterile' space in which to observe the remains of the body. Bodies would enter the mortuary via the grandstand tunnel. There was also a separate entrance to the mortuary for the bodies of those who died as a result of chemical weapons. Bodies entering the morgue via this route would be processed in a sluicing space created by roofing over an area next to the grandstand. The sluicing room provided a safe space to decontaminate the bodies before they entered the morgue. A new door was also knocked through into an outbuilding which provided the mortuary staff access to baths and changing facilities. Behind the mortuary, provision was also made for an ambulance by constructing a garage. At a meeting of the Civil Defence Emergency Committee held on 2 February 1943, the town clerk submitted an approval of the Senior Regional Officer to spend £327.17s.6d to make alterations to the emergency mortuary at the grandstand, which superseded the £325.4s.6d that was authorised on 22 December 1942. It is unknown what alterations were subsequently made to the grandstand with this additional funding.

To transport bodies to the emergency mortuary, the local authority provided two buses that, in April 1941, were stationed at the Corporation Transport Department. At the meeting of the Civil Defence Emergency Committee held on 7 April 1941, the town clerk reported that difficulties had arisen in arranging for the drivers of these vehicles when they were needed. It was the town clerk's recommendation that the buses should be placed under the control of the Ambulance Officer and moved to the service depot. At this meeting the Ambulance Officer also reported that it would be possible, with minor alterations, to convert the buses into temporary ambulances and use them for mortuary purposes when they were not needed for treating the injured. The Committee approved the recommendations, and the buses were transferred to the Ambulance Officer. Following suggestions by the Ministry of Health on 21 June 1941, the committee also approved that the mortuary vehicles should be fitted out with linoleum so they could be easily cleaned after use.

In March 1943, Lincoln's emergency mortuary service failed to operate effectively during the Civil Defence GAMMA exercise. The main issue faced by the emergency mortuary during the exercise was a breakdown in communication, and the lack of vehicles. It was the opinion of the Civil Defence Committee that the breakdown in service was the result of the strain under which the emergency mortuary superintendent operated, exacerbated by the fact that they had no deputy with detailed local knowledge. On reminding the superintendent of their responsibilities, the Civil Defence Committee considered that no further difficulties should arise. During the GAMMA exercise, the mobile canteen also failed to visit the emergency mortuary. The committee subsequently put in place arrangements to ensure that light refreshments would be delivered to the emergency mortuary as soon as possible after bombs started being dropped on Lincoln.

On 25 October 1944, the town clerk received a circular from the Senior Regional Officer, Ministry of Health, stating that the Ministry had considered the question of reducing the emergency mortuary service, but decided that there was still a need to operate emergency mortuaries. The Ministry also notified the town clerk that one fully equipped mortuary would be sufficient for each town with a population of over 40,000, and the emergency mortuary at the grandstand would, therefore, be retained for the time being. The precise date that the emergency mortuary at the grandstand closed is unknown.

The processing of the dead during the Second World War has received very little attention. Despite adapting a racecourse grandstand, the design and layout of Lincoln's emergency mortuary provided spaces both for the living and the dead. The mortuary provided a space in which friends and relatives could identify their loved ones, as well as an area in which the bereaved could grieve and start to come to terms with their loss.

Grandstand, Saxilby Road. (*Andrew Walker*).

Lincoln's World War Memorials I: Bracebridge, Boultham and St Benedict's Square

Andrew Walker and Arthur Ward

Three prominent public memorials were constructed within the contemporary boundaries of the city in honour of those who died in the Great War of 1914–18. Names were added to these structures following the war of 1939–45, in some cases with references to the Great War removed and the terms First and Second World War employed to identify the two periods of conflict.

In addition to these memorials, many other structures, often tablets with the names of the dead, were unveiled across the city, mainly in places of work and worship, but also on occasion in sites of sporting and political activity. In this chapter, attention is paid particularly to memorialising those Lincoln inhabitants who died in action but were not buried in the city. In its consideration of First World War memorialisation, it draws upon Michael Credland's extensive volume, *The First World War Memorials of Lincolnshire*.

After much parliamentary debate at the outset of the First World War, it was determined that Britain's war dead should be buried near to where they fell, rather than undertaking the complex task of repatriating the bodies and returning them to their families. The Imperial (later Commonwealth) War Graves Commission was set up to oversee the construction and maintenance of these cemeteries. It was also decided that, in death, there should be equality amongst the military. The gravestones installed in Britain's war cemeteries, designed by Edwin Lutyens, with the distinctive lettering of Leslie MacDonald Gill, were to be uniform of design, notwithstanding the rank or social standing of the combatant buried. This equality in death was generally a philosophy followed in the listing of names on war memorials in Britain, where, usually, names were ordered alphabetically by surname, or by date of death.

Bracebridge War Memorial

Until 9 November 1920, Bracebridge parish was located outside the boundaries of the city. Thus, at the time of the war memorial's unveiling on Saturday 6 November 1920, this was not a city of Lincoln memorial. Its original site was next to the village school. Following realignment of the road junction, the memorial was removed in 1970 and relocated several yards away, though still at the junction of Maple Street and Newark Road. This was amongst the first of the county's war memorials to be unveiled. It is built of Portland stone, with red granite panels containing the names of the 45 war dead – 39 of whose names were inscribed

The relocated Bracebridge war memorial, at the junction of Newark Road and Maple Street. (*Andrew Walker*).

at the time of its unveiling – and was supplemented by a further 31 names after the Second World War, though these were only added in 1994. This was one of many war memorials built by the Lincoln firm of Messrs M. Tuttell and Son. As with many of the First World War memorials, originally low-level iron railings surrounded the structure but were removed and melted down during the Second World War.

Boultham War Memorial

A plaque containing the names of Boultham's First World War dead was unveiled in St Helen's Church in November 1920. The parish's war memorial was unveiled three years later at the junction of Boultham Park Road and Dixon Street. The structure was of Portland stone with a Gothic cross. It contained the names of 53 men who were killed in action. An additional 40 names were inscribed in the base of the monument in 1949, representing those who perished in the 1939–45 conflict. A local sculptor, Harry Jackson designed and produced the memorial, which, in common with many such examples, was funded by local voluntary contributions.

From the outset, the location of the memorial at a busy junction caused some access problems. In 1923, the sharpness of the corner between the two roads at the memorial was

Boultham war memorial, situated at the junction of Dixon Street and Boultham Park Road. (*Andrew Walker*).

rounded, making the junction a little less dangerous. In part to mark the 50th anniversary of the end of the Second World War, the structure was refurbished and landscaped in 1995 by the City of Lincoln Council's Planning and Architecture Department.

City of Lincoln War Memorial, St Benedict's Square

Much debate took place regarding the location of the city's public war memorial. Various locations were considered, including on the Cornhill, and outside the Sessions House, on the north-east corner of the junction between Broadgate and Monks Road. Initially, it was hoped that Sir Reginald Blomfield could be commissioned to design the structure. His previous work in the city had included the Westgate Water Tower and the Central Library. Later he would design the Usher Gallery, and a number of substantial international war memorials, including the Menin Gate at Ypres.

In 1919, Blomfield produced a design for a 40-feet high stone obelisk to be situated on the Cornhill, facing the High Street. The project's likely cost of approximately £10,000 led to its abandonment. Bloomfield produced an alternative plan, including what was described in the *Lincolnshire Echo* on 15 May 1920 as 'a noble and inspiring' design, with a bronze winged figure of Victory on a Portland stone pedestal, with a dying soldier lying across her feet. The estimate

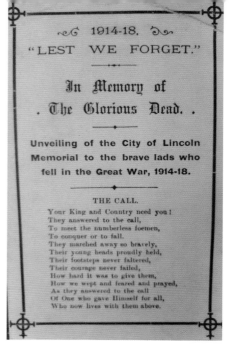

The proposed city centre war memorial in Cornhill, designed by Sir Reginald Blomfield, 1919. (*Courtesy of Lincoln Central Library, Lincolnshire County Council/GLL. Ref. 603*).

A card commemorating the unveiling of the city centre war memorial on Wednesday 25 October 1922. (*Courtesy of Lincoln Central Library, Lincolnshire County Council/GLL. Ref. 8512*).

for the work was c. £6000, and it soon became clear that public subscriptions would not be able to raise this sum. A Blomfield-designed war memorial does, however, exist in the city – the cross of sacrifice, in Newport Cemetery where it forms the centrepiece of the war graves plot. Similar crosses, designed by Blomfield in 1918, can be found in war cemeteries across the world.

The local press criticised the city's slowness to construct a civic memorial, pointing to how 'Bracebridge got a move on while Lincoln lagged behind'. Later war memorial fund-raising endeavours, included a 'grand ladies' football match' between Boston and Lincoln at Sincil Bank on Armistice Day, 1921, and house-to-house collections. By April 1922, through some 12,000 individual donations, a total of £3200 was raised.

Finally, a more modest design was agreed and an acceptable site was secured by the Corporation, when it acquired 172 square yards of St Benedict's churchyard, between the church and the High Street. As part of the terms of the sale, it was agreed that the Corporation would pay for the reburial of any human remains disturbed during the construction work. The tasks of design and construction were assigned to a range of Lincoln-based individuals and firms: Captain Montague Ashley Hall was the responsible architect; A.J. Tuttell, the sculptor; William Wright & Sons, the builders; and Charles Roberts manufactured the surrounding wrought-iron gates and railings, which, as with those at Bracebridge memorial, were removed during the Second World War.

Hall's design emphasised the locality. It was inspired by the Eleanor crosses which had been built to mark the body of Queen Eleanor's journey from Lincoln Cathedral, where she was briefly laid to rest following her death at nearby Harby, to Westminster Abbey in 1290. Lincoln's original Eleanor Cross, located at Swine Green, at the bottom of Cross O'Cliff Hill, had long since disappeared, though a fragment of the cross is now located in the grounds of Lincoln Castle. Local Ancaster stone was the material used for the 36-feet tall, highly-decorated Gothic style structure, with its four buttresses and octagonal base. A total of 973 names appeared on the monument, which was unveiled on Wednesday 25 October 1922

A crowd surrounding the city centre war memorial, with fresh wreaths visible on its base, c.1925. (*Courtesy of Lincoln Central Library, Lincolnshire County Council/GLL. Ref. LCL1171*).

by the senior Lincolnshire military figure, Field Marshal Sir William Robertson, who also received the freedom of the city on the day. In his much-reported speech at the memorial he suggested that the war might have been shortened if politicians had not intervened in military operations.

Following the Second World War, considerable delay occurred before the names of 314 individuals who had lost their lives were added to the memorial. By 1948, complaints were being made that inscribing the names of the Second World War dead to the war memorial

The city centre war memorial in St Benedict's Square. (*Andrew Walker*).

was being 'too long delayed'; on 4 March 1952, the *Lincolnshire Echo* remarked that adding the names had been 'permanently pigeonholed'. Finally, just before remembrance commemorations in November 1955, over ten years after the end of hostilities, Lincoln's war memorial was brought up to date with the names added and the inscription on its front was altered from 'the Great War, 1914–18' to 'in the First and Second World Wars'.

A further unveiling of the memorial took place in October 2005, 60 years after the end of the Second World War, following a six-week refurbishment process, during which a ramp was installed to enable those with physical disabilities to access the monument.

Lincoln's World War Memorials II: Other memorials to the city's war dead

Andrew Walker and Arthur Ward

In contrast to the slowness of remembering Lincoln's war dead in a physical form on a city-wide level, there were many smaller memorials installed quite soon after hostilities ended. This chapter is by no means an exhaustive list of these memorials but seeks to demonstrate the extent of this commemoration and of course the depth of mourning felt across the city following these war losses. Many places of worship were amongst the first to install memorials to those killed after the First World War, the majority of whom could not be buried in the city. These included the soldiers' memorial unveiled in the Cathedral's Soldiers' Chapel in May 1919 and stone tablets unveiled in 1920 at the churches of St Mary le Wigford, St Paul in the Bail and St Helen, Boultham. At St Mary Magdalene, a 'war shrine' was erected, in memory of 'those lads of the parish from whom war exacted their lives'. This was made of teakwood from the battleship 'Britannia'. M. Tuttell and Son was commissioned to design and build several memorials, including the West Parade Wesleyan Church's memorial tablet in 1923. In 1920, A.J. Tuttell produced the Lincoln Mission Church war memorial on Vernon Street. St Faith's war memorial, completed in 1923, comprised a large tablet of English oak, and contained the names of 90 men of the West End parish who had been killed. The war memorial in the church of St Nicholas, unveiled in April 1923, composed of an impressive three-panelled, carved-oak reredos, with a centre panel featuring a crucifixion scene. It contained the 139 names of parishioners. A 14 feet-high Portland stone crucifix in St Andrew's churchyard, commemorated 58 of its parishioners.

In addition to tablets, and other wooden and stone structures, stained glass was also used to memorialise the dead. Two windows were installed in 1924 in Lincoln Cathedral's St George's chapel in memory of the men of Lincolnshire and the Lincolnshire Regiment who gave their lives in the Great War. This was the work of Archibald Nicholson and was inspired by the Cathedral's thirteenth-century stained glass. Several years earlier, in 1920, a stained glass window was unveiled in the church of St Peter in Eastgate with St Margaret in honour of 25 parishioners killed.

Memorialisation after the First World War also occurred beyond the city's churches and chapels. Amongst schools who remembered their former pupils who had died was the city's Municipal Technical School, which constructed a memorial designed by its own pupils, in honour of the 70 old boys of the school who died in action. The Lincoln Constitutional Club erected a memorial tablet to its young members. It was situated in the entrance hall to the building. Its rival, the Liberal Club, also installed a memorial plaque in honour of its dead

In Honoured Memory of their Colleagues, who gave their lives in the Great War 1914-1919.

GOODS DEPT.
JOSEPH EDWARD AYRES
ALBERT CODLING
CYRIL COLE
PERCY WILLIAM SANDERS
EDWIN WHITTAKER

PASSENGER DEPT.
FRANK HOLLOWAY
GEORGE HOLLOWAY
ROBERT WILLIAM KERSHAW
JOSEPH WHITELAM

LOCO DEPT.
JOHN HIND, GEORGE WILLIAM SMITH.

A memorial plaque to 11 Midland Railway staff who died in the First World War and now located on platform one of Lincoln railway station, which used to be operated by the Great Northern Railway. (*Andrew Walker*).

members. Lincoln County Hospital was the site of a memorial tablet for the Lincolnshire Yeomanry, which was unveiled in 1922, alongside a new x-ray department and pathology laboratory as a memorial for the fallen. Having been confined to an outbuilding for many years, the various sections of the plaque were brought together, re-dedicated and installed in the haematology department waiting room in 2012, thanks in large part to the work of Michael Credland. At places of work, memorials were also commissioned and conspicuously located. The Royal Insurance Society listed its employees from across its Lincoln branches who had fallen on a bronze tablet in the entrance hall to its main branch in the city. Lincoln City's two police officers who were killed in action were remembered in a memorial in the police headquarters in the Sessions House on Monks Road. A marble tablet bearing the names of the eleven Midland Railway staff from Lincoln who had died was unveiled at the Midland station. It has since been relocated from St Mark's to the surviving Lincoln Central Railway Station. Lincoln's Great Northern Railway staff who died are listed on the company's national war memorial, refurbished and reinstated in 2013, which is located at King's Cross Station. At a ceremony attended by the mayor and the Bishop of Lincoln, a bronze tablet was unveiled in Lincoln's General Post Office on Guildhall Street in February

1921, with the names of 21 employees killed during the war. A newspaper account of the ceremony listed three other postal workers who died of their wounds after the war; their names, it stated, would be added later. However, this does not appear to have taken place. A smaller brass plaque was added after the Second World War recording the names of the eight employees killed during this conflict. The Post Office plaques were moved from the Guildhall Street building to Sincil Street following the service's relocation. However, they are not on public view in the city centre's Post Office at its current location in the Stonebow Centre on Silver Street.

Perhaps one of the most heart-rending First World War memorial plaques in the city is that which was unveiled in 2019 in The Arboretum, in honour of the five Beechey brothers all of whom were killed in action during the war in separate locations, aged at death between 39 and 26 years. Their mother, Amy, lived on nearby Avondale Road, and is buried in Newport Cemetery.

Many of the inscriptions on the memorials installed after the First World War were extended after the 1939–45 conflict to include the names of these additional fatalities. In some instances, organisations that had not previously commissioned memorials for their First World War dead did so after 1945. In October 1948, for instance, Lincoln's YMCA installed

A plaque remembering the five Beechey brothers who were killed during the First World War, which was unveiled at The Arboretum, on Monks Road in 2019. (*Andrew Walker*).

A memorial to the air crews and ground staff of 50 and 61 squadrons, based at RAF Skellingthorpe, situated on Birchwood Avenue. (*Andrew Walker*).

a plaque on a wall by the entrance hall at its headquarters remembering its members who had died in both world wars.

Unsurprisingly, memorials at current or former military sites to the dead of the two world wars can also be found in the city. The first of these to appear, in September 1920, was an extensive tablet listing those who lost their lives amongst the volunteers of the Fourth Battalion Lincolnshire Regiment which was erected at the Drill Hall, designed by Captain Montague A. Hall, and manufactured by Messrs Tuttell & Son. This was supplemented by another plaque after the 1939–45 conflict. During the restoration of the Drill Hall, a wooden memorial was found in the basement rifle range and, at the building's reopening in 2006, was placed more conspicuously in the café area, at the western end of the refurbished building. At the Sobraon Barracks on Burton Road, a memorial to the Lincolnshire Regiment was installed in 2012 in Sobraon Park. This substantial brick-built structure, echoes the building materials used in the barracks built in 1890. Within the structure, two of the memorial plaques listing the war dead, previously housed in the barracks, were incorporated.

The lives lost in the Second World War by members of the Royal Air Force locally are remembered in another relatively recently erected memorial to the air crews and ground staff of 50 and 61 squadrons who were based at RAF Skellingthorpe. A memorial to them, erected in 1989, stands on what was part of the airbase and which is now Birchwood Avenue. On Castle Hill, next to the castle's eastern wall, the Parachute Regimental Association Airborne Memorial

Garden remembers the sacrifices of those who served in the RAF. This was opened in September 1989 and includes a polished, inscribed granite column.

Despite the memorials' general exhortations to remember, in several cases not all of them in Lincoln have survived. Perhaps the most dramatic loss was that of the Portland stone war memorial cross in St Andrew's churchyard on Portland Street, which was demolished on Good Friday, 1954. The 58 names memorialised on this structure were later engraved on a brass plaque which is now situated in the lobby of Dunston House on Portland Street, near the site of the original war memorial and the now-demolished church. Particularly prone to destruction were memorial tablets and plaques, though, as Michael Credland has observed, some of these have been rescued, such as the plaque in Silver Street Methodist Chapel, which was found buried in a garden in Cherry Willingham and later installed in All Saints Church on Monks Road; and the memorial tablet from the Wesleyan Chapel on Clasketgate, which was later found in the cellar of Bailgate Methodist Church, where it was then placed in the entrance porch.

The entrance door to the Parachute Regimental Association's airborne memorial garden, next to the castle's eastern wall, on Castle Hill. (*Andrew Walker*).

Given the loss, or temporary mislaying, of a number of these structures, there seems to be a need for a definitive list of the city's surviving world war memorials in order to aid the continued honouring of the city's world war dead.

Lincoln Undertakers

Adam Cartwright

The term 'undertaker' originally had a more general meaning: anybody who was prepared to take on a range of tasks that might need some degree of skill or organisation could call themselves a general undertaker. The notion of a specific funeral undertaker had, however, existed since the early 1700s; having somebody co-ordinate the necessary arrangements slowly became popular with upper and middle class families who could afford to pay for the service. John Cheney of Boston advertised his 'willingness to serve any Funeral at reasonable Rates' in the *Stamford Mercury* in September 1725.

Elaborate funeral processions and ceremonies are often thought of as peculiarly Victorian practices. Certainly, a wider fascination with death became widespread in the era, but, as early as 1811, the funeral of Lady Jane Edwards at Welham, Leicestershire, undertaken by Henry Weldon of Stamford, attracted a long procession to the church, 'with the body in a hearse, drawn by six horses, richly dressed with Feathers, velvets, escutcheons, Streamers, Pendants…'

Demonstrating that the undertaking trade was often ancillary to other businesses, Lincoln's main undertakers for many years were the home furnishers Curtis & Mawer. In 1868 Edmund Curtis moved his cabinet-making business from 228 High Street (later part of the Mawer & Collingham department store and then House of Fraser) to more commodious premises at 40 Silver Street, where he took over the furniture warehouse of the retiring George Wilson. Employing the woodworking skills he had learned, Curtis started an undertaker's at the rear of his new furnishing store, which became Lincoln's main funeral business for many years. In 1890, Curtis's son went into partnership with Fred Mawer, establishing the Curtis & Mawer business. The undertakers' side of the operation was managed and considerably expanded by Fred Mawer, who died in his early forties in 1908, managing funerals for many of the city's key business people. A particularly unusual funeral was that of circus proprietor Thomas Transfield, once of Lincoln, who died in the United States in 1911. His body was repatriated to Curtis & Mawer's for burial at Canwick Cemetery: according to a former employee, a huge packing case arrived containing the body, in a coffin, dressed in a ringmaster's outfit complete with top hat and whip.

So successful was the business that the premises were completely rebuilt in the late 1890s as a three-storey, four-bay building, featuring a white terracotta facade and large plate-glass windows in department store classical style. Badly damaged by a devastating fire in February 1922, the business operated from temporary premises for just over a year, which must have been extremely difficult for the funerals trade.

5 QUEEN STREET, LINCOLN

The Executors of the late Wm. Spacey.

Dr. to Fullalove Bros.

JOINERS AND BUILDERS.

SPECIALISTS IN HORTICULTURAL WORK.   SHOP AND OFFICE FITTINGS, Etc.

PHONE 412.   ESTABLISHED 1860.

Headed stationery of Fullalove Bros, 1919. The invoice is for a funeral, but it seems that undertaking does not feature prominently in the company's marketing. (*Courtesy of Jonathan Whiting*).

The (now defunct) national chain Court's bought the premises in 1972 but were not interested in taking on the undertaking side of Curtis & Mawer, which therefore ceased trading. Following Courts UK's collapse in 2004, the premises are now occupied by the Taste Oriental Buffet and a snooker hall, but two C&M logos can still be seen at the top of the facade, just underneath the cornice, with the date, 1922, commemorating the fire.

At the other end of the scale were working-class funerals. The expense of such ceremonies was well beyond the means of most people, for whom death at home rather than in hospital was very commonplace; unless there was any prospect of immediate medical intervention, accident victims were almost always taken back to their homes, where a doctor might attend to make them as comfortable as possible. For the very poor or destitute, the cost of at least some level of respectable treatment after death fell on the local Board of Guardians or local parish officers, most of whom sought annual tenders for the supply of coffins for pauper burials. Most of those bidding were joiners or builders, supposedly skilled in working with wood but not necessarily having the skills needed for an undertaker. Some undoubtedly felt that they could get away with poor quality work for pauper funerals; in 1871 a Grimsby priest, George Johnson, on giving a coffin lid a gentle pull, was horrified to find it readily yield to the pressure and the black features of the decomposing corpse exposed to view. This was not an isolated case.

George Thorpe, a 25-year-old builder, was given a coffin contract by the Lincoln Board of Guardians in 1877. By 1881, he was bankrupt but was still supplying the Board a year later

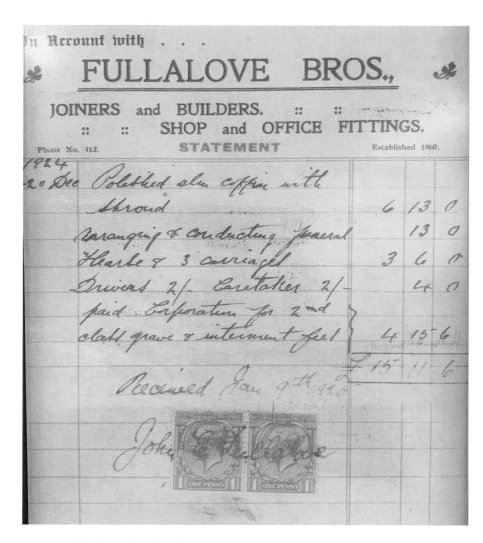

An invoice for a funeral conducted in December 1924 by Fullalove Bros of Queen Street. Details include a polished elm coffin with shroud, a hearse and three carriages, and payment to the Corporation for a second-class grave. (*Courtesy of Jonathan Whiting*).

and disputing the price he could charge for coffin nameplates. Worse was to come: by 1888 the coffin contract was with a blacksmith and wheelwright, George Kew of Waldeck Street, whose frequent disputes with customers in the civil courts were well publicised. The Board clearly considered him a fit and proper person – until his involvement in the Saxilby burial scandal. Mary Kennedy died in March 1900, leaving her six children orphans, and because she was receiving poor relief, the village authorities had to meet the cost of her funeral. Kew agreed to act as undertaker, but arrived twenty minutes late for the funeral and, according to the vicar, the body was bundled into the coffin which was too small, and because no bearers had been engaged, two nearby gardeners agreed to help out at very short notice. Eighteen months later, Kew again was late providing a coffin, this time to the Lincoln mortuary, incurring the displeasure of the Lincoln coroner Alexander Trotter. On this occasion, Kew admitted his tardiness and the Board members voted – only just – to rescind his contract. Remarkably, by 1903, he was again managing funerals for the Board, suggesting that their main interest was keeping costs as low as possible rather than respecting the dead.

Kew was by no means one of the worst examples in the county, but changes were coming to the profession. The term 'funeral director', meaning one who arranged all aspects of a funeral rather than just building a coffin, seems to have been first used around 1882, and, by February 1884, Edwin Cansdale of the Economical Funeral Depot in Cross Street was describing himself thus. Cremations, too, were becoming more popular amongst the middle classes, despite the opposition of the Bishop of Lincoln (1869–85), Christopher Wordsworth, who declared in 1874 that he could not think of anything more barbarous and unnatural, thereby earning himself widespread ridicule.

The first crematorium in the UK was opened at Brookwood, near Woking, in 1879, followed in 1892 by another at Manchester, but demand remained low for many years. By the time Thomas King, the proprietor of the Lincoln Theatre Royal, was cremated at Manchester in 1903, the fourth from Lincolnshire to be received at the crematorium, just under two services a week were taking place there. It continued to be difficult to arrange a local cremation until November 1968, when Lincoln Crematorium opened on Washingborough Road. This is the subject of a chapter by Andrew Walker.

Two of Lincoln's current funeral directors have been operating for over 50 years. The Lincolnshire Co-operative Society is the oldest, having arranged funerals since at least 1890. Its funeral department was located at 12 Portland Street from 1930 until 2015, when a new build (and highly impressive) funeral home was opened on a site on Tritton Road at a cost of £2 million. The Society owns another site at Proctors Road in the north of the city and a further 18 sites across the county.

Another business with some history to it is Priestley & Cockett, of Sunningdale Drive, just off Boultham Park Road. It was formed in 1966 when Len Cockett, an undertaker since the late 1940s, went into partnership with T. A. Priestley, who had taken over the long-established funeral business of Herbert Threadgold in 1960. Threadgold had been an undertaker for over 50 years, trading from 68 Bailgate, where his wife ran a women's underwear shop. The Bailgate premises closed in the 1980s and the business was acquired by the national funerals' provider, Dignity plc, who own about 800 other funeral directors, cemeteries and crematoria.

The independent funeral director Jonathan Whiting, who has premises at 1–5 Queen Street, considers the more recent history of funerals in his later chapter. Part of Mr Whiting's property, number 5, had for many years been associated with the undertaking trade: the Fullalove Brothers occupied the premises from 1892, taking over from their father who had been in business since 1860. At least from 1892 until 1938, in addition to their work as horticultural and general builders, the Fullalove Brothers' advertisements declared that their services from this address also included 'funerals furnished'. It seems, then, that, until at least the end of the inter-war period, undertaking funerals was often an ancillary part of several Lincoln businesses' operations.

A Funeral Carriage Supplier

Geoff Tann

In addition to undertakers and funeral directors, Lincoln supported a more specialised firm that appears to have been concerned with transport provision for both the deceased and the mourners. George Cullen, the son of a chimney sweep, briefly worked in the Ruston & Hornsby forge and a skin yard, married. joined his father as a sweep, and then established himself as a hansom cab driver based at 10 The Park. When a fare left £400 in his cab after a horse race in 1895, George dutifully handed it in to local police who returned it to the jockey (who had only declared a £300 loss). The finder was entitled to a reward of £2 under Lincoln byelaws but the Mayor suggested that Cullen might be 'handsomely rewarded' by the jockey.

If that reward was made, it could explain how Cullen was able to start a funeral carriage sideline by 1899 with two of his brothers assisting him. He placed a newspaper advertisement in November 1904; such was his confidence that he bought premises at 20 Carholme Road for £330 in December and moved the business there. By 1910 he was also operating from 38 Carholme Road, eventually providing up to ten black horses when required. His sons joined the firm by 1939; his daughter Gladys returned from America in 1940 to play an active part driving hearses donned with a top hat but never featured in the firm's name. Plumed horses were apparently rarely part of Lincoln funerals, Gladys recalled in 1960, except for their Gypsy clients. George Cullen died in 1945, leaving the company to his sons and daughter.

The last reported funeral catered for by the company was in 1959. By 1960 the horse-drawn element had declined considerably, leaving racks of top hats and frock coats in the hall of Gladys's home at 38 Carholme Road. Cullen's Limousine Service continued until 1980 when the siblings retired and it was taken over by West End Motors (based at the Winning Post service station).

Some of the premises associated with these three former businesses still exist but mostly in much-altered condition. Former stables and later motor car garages remain in Harvey Street from George Cullen's business, as do the properties at 20 and 38 Carholme Road, now in residential use.

A contemporary horse-drawn hearse. (*Courtesy of Jonathan Whiting*).

Four Victorian Funerals: Dr Charlesworth, Bishop Wordsworth, Mrs Bromhead and Joseph Ruston

Lesley Church

The four funerals described in this chapter are of figures significant in Lincoln in the nineteenth century: Edward Parker Charlesworth, the physician who paved the way for the non-restraint system at Lincoln Lunatic Asylum; Christopher Wordsworth, Bishop of Lincoln; Mrs Anne Bromhead, pioneer of nursing services in Lincoln and Lincolnshire; and Joseph Ruston, industrialist and benefactor. In addition to their gravestones, there are memorials to three of the four: a statue of Dr Charlesworth; an altar-tomb in Lincoln Cathedral for Bishop Wordsworth; and a hospital in memory of Mrs Bromhead. Joseph Ruston's name lived on in the factories and machinery bearing his name, a ward at Lincoln County Hospital, and the Drill Hall on Broadgate which he financed.

Dr Edward Parker Charlesworth, Physician

Dr Charlesworth was physician to the County Hospital and to Lincoln Lunatic Asylum. He set in motion the move towards the non-restraint system of care in the Asylum which Robert Gardiner Hill later introduced fully, and which Dr John Conolly of Hanwell Asylum in Middlesex adopted, leading to the system's spread and acceptance throughout the country.

Dr Charlesworth died in 1853 and was buried in St Margaret's churchyard not far from his home at 4 Pottergate. Only a few close relatives, and the doctor who had looked after him in his last illness, attended his private funeral, but afterwards a large crowd of mourners gathered round the grave to pay their respects. Shops were closed and a muffled peal of bells sounded from St Peter-at-Arches church.

An unostentatious gravestone in St Margaret's churchyard commemorates both Dr Charlesworth and his wife Susannah who died in 1854. Measures were quickly in progress to provide a public testimonial to his memory. A statue was decided upon and Thomas Milnes, whose work already included a statue of Wellington and one of Nelson, was chosen as the sculptor. His statue, of white Sicilian marble on a Yorkshire granite plinth, stands in the grounds of The Lawn, on the corner of Carline Road and Union Road. The statue was unveiled at an inauguration in July 1854, at which Dr John Conolly was one of the speakers.

Christopher Wordsworth, Bishop of Lincoln

Christopher Wordsworth was consecrated Bishop of Lincoln in 1869 and lived in the Bishop's Palace at Riseholme with his family. He died on 20 March 1885, just a few months after his wife's death and shortly after resigning through ill health, while staying at his daughter's home in Harewood, Yorkshire. His funeral took place in Lincoln Cathedral on 25 March, but he was buried in the churchyard at Riseholme next to his wife.

His body was brought to Lincoln by train from Leeds. At the Cathedral, students of the Theological College carried the coffin from the south porch to the Morning Prayer Chapel. The lid of the coffin was removed, and many came to have a last look at his face. The funeral service in the Choir the next day – which was the day of the Lincoln Races, but the races ceased during the time of the funeral – was a choral service with lessons read by Ven. Archdeacon Kaye. 'Hark! The sound of holy voices', written by Bishop Wordsworth, was sung. After the service, according to the bishop's biographers, J. H. Overton and Elizabeth Wordsworth, 'the flower-covered coffin followed by the mourners two and two' passed between the 'closely-packed throngs of spectators, through the west door to be conveyed to Riseholme'. At the graveside, Archdeacon Kaye and the Archbishop of Canterbury read the burial service. The grave had been

Statue of Dr Charlesworth at The Lawn. (*Lesley Church*).

lined with ivy, mosses and daffodils, with blue and white violets around the sides. A cross of grey Irish limestone was later erected over the graves with medallions carved with types and antitypes of the Old and New Testament. The medallions are much eroded now and the cracked cross is supported by a metal rod.

The monument to Christopher Wordsworth, designed by Thomas Garner, is in the Angel Choir of Lincoln Cathedral. The bishop reposes under a canopy on an altar-tomb, and pierces a dragon at his feet with his staff. The base is decorated with arches containing statues of the apostles, and the canopy is surmounted by the figure of Christ.

St Margaret's churchyard, where Dr Charlesworth is buried. (*Lesley Church*).

Anne Fector Bromhead, founder and superintendent of the Lincoln Institution for Nurses

Mrs Bromhead, daughter of George Ralph Payne Jarvis of Doddington Hall, was responsible for the improvement of nursing services in Lincoln and Lincolnshire. From the beginning of her mission in 1864, her purpose was twofold: to improve nursing at Lincoln's County Hospital and to provide a nursing service beyond the hospital to rich and poor in city and county. The partnership with the hospital was short-lived and fraught with problems, but the nursing service provided by the Institution for Trained Nurses, which she established and managed, thrived.

Anne Bromhead died in April 1886. Her funeral took place at Canwick Road Cemetery. The *Lincolnshire Chronicle* (16 April 1886) listed only gentlemen mourners, although 30 of her nurses, who had known her as 'Lady Mother' came to the graveside, each with a bunch of snowdrops to lay round the edges of the grave. It was not considered acceptable during the early and mid-Victorian era for ladies of the upper and middle classes to attend

The three Bromhead crosses in Canwick Road Cemetery. (*Lesley Church*).

a funeral as it was thought they would be unable to contain their emotions and would disrupt the solemnity of the service with their sobs. Even in the 1880s *Cassell's Household Guide* continued to advise that women should not attend, though in 1884 the Wordsworth daughters were present at their mother's funeral with their father, and Joseph Ruston's wife and daughters attended his funeral in 1897. Mrs Bromhead was buried by the side of her husband, later to be joined by her daughter Henrietta, who carried on her mother's work until her own death in 1907, and son Charles. Three simple crosses mark their graves.

In October 1886 a meeting was held at the home of industrialist Nathaniel Clayton to consider a memorial in recognition of Mrs Bromhead's services to the community. It was decided that this should be of benefit to Mrs Bromhead's Institution for Nurses, and it was proposed that the memorial should be a sanatorium. The building, designed by William Watkins, on the corner of Church Lane and Nettleham Road, originally known as the Red House, then The Bromhead, and now the Lincoln Hospital, stands as a tribute to Mrs Bromhead.

Joseph Ruston, Industrialist and Benefactor

Joseph Ruston, head of the firm of Ruston, Proctor & Co. at the Sheaf Ironworks in Lincoln, died in June 1897. His funeral took place at St Peter-in-Eastgate Church, and he was buried in St Peter-in-Eastgate cemetery, separate from the church, by the side of his eldest daughter Alice.

A short service was held in the Rustons' home, Monks Manor (between Wragby Road and Greetwell Road) for the family, a few friends, and the deacons of Newland Congregational Church where Joseph Ruston had himself been a deacon for over thirty years, before the cortege set out on the road to St Peter-in-Eastgate Church. The funeral cortege was joined by the Mayor and Sheriff, magistrates and Corporation, and others followed including Alfred Shuttleworth, officers of the Lincoln Sunday School Union, representatives of the Mechanics' Institute, YMCA, Lincoln Temperance Society, members of local firms, local tradesmen, railway officials and many private citizens. The men of the Sheaf Works lined the route which was 'thronged with people, many deep' (*Stamford Mercury* 18 June 1897).

The Sheaf Works Band, wearing white gloves and crape armlets, headed the procession, playing Handel's 'Dead March' from *Saul*. The coffin was covered in wreaths and borne in a glass-panelled hearse with about 100 men from the Sheaf Works accompanying the hearse carrying floral tributes. The principal mourners followed in coaches, including Mrs Ruston and the Miss Rustons, and about 20 other carriages followed with eminent members of Lincoln society.

The Bishop was already in the church. During the funeral, the Cathedral bell and St Peter-in-Eastgate's church bell tolled. Afterwards a half-muffled peal was rung on the bells of St Peter-at-Arches. Many shops were closed. In St Peter-in-Eastgate cemetery, the Ruston vault, in the south-east corner, was adorned with evergreens and white pinks. The family must have been reminded of the burial of daughter Alice as they stood by the grave for the burial of her father. Alice's hearse had been preceded by six men servants and eight women servants bearing wreaths, and either side of the hearse 15 foremen from the Sheaf Works with wreaths. Ten carriages had followed. Her grave had been lined with moss and flowers. (*Stamford Mercury* 29 June 1888). Flowers were an important feature of the celebration of a funeral, then as now, softening the bleakness of the event with their colours and scents, and lining the base of the grave with moss and flowers was an attempt to disguise the harsh reality of the bare earth. A beautifully carved cross marks the grave not only of Joseph Ruston but also his daughter Alice and his wife Jane. Gary Rook's later chapter considers the recent restoration of this monument.

Victorian funerals could be extravagant and ostentatious, particularly those of the upper and middle classes, but none of these funerals could be described in this way. Dr Charlesworth's funeral was a very private one, and those of Bishop Wordsworth and Mrs Bromhead seem to have been conducted with dignity and simplicity. Only Joseph Ruston's funeral was in any way a spectacle, with its glass-panelled hearse, long procession of mourners in carriages and on foot, and the Sheaf Works Band, but all the funerals brought local people into the streets or to the cemetery to pay their respects.

Graves of Lincoln's Nineteenth-Century Mayors

Ken Redmore

The men who took the office of Mayor of Lincoln in the late nineteenth century were from a variety of backgrounds and occupations. In broad terms they were either leaders in local industry or commerce or from one of the professions. Their origins were varied too: about one third were born in Lincoln and the remainder, in roughly equal numbers, were from elsewhere in Lincolnshire or from further afield in England. Nevertheless, with few exceptions, all these men lived and worked in the city for much of their lives; they also spent their years of retirement there and were buried in one of the city cemeteries.

This brief study examines the memorials which mark the graves of 22 men who served as mayors in Lincoln during the second half of the nineteenth century. The majority of them were buried in the Canwick Road Old Cemetery; a smaller number are to be found in Eastgate Cemetery.

As might be expected, some of the memorials to former mayors are large and impressive. Nathaniel Clayton (Mayor 1856, died 1890), the agricultural engineer of international renown, has a striking pink granite memorial over his grave on a prominent corner site in the Canwick Road Cemetery. There is no other monument in this style in the cemetery – a tall pedestal topped by graduated spire – and few match its height (3.6m). Bronze panels, now coated in green verdigris, carry his name in raised lettering. As with many other memorials in this survey, Nathaniel Clayton's name appears alongside other members of his family – in this instance, parents, sister, brother-in-law, nephew, wife, daughter and son-in-law are given equal prominence.

The memorial over Joseph Ruston's grave (M.1869, d.1897) in Eastgate Cemetery is equally impressive, though of entirely different design. It is in the form of richly decorated cross in Celtic style, 2.9m in height, mounted on a short pedestal. Both the monument and the kerb which surrounds the grave are fabricated from white marble, and the whole assemblage has been given an outstandingly fresh appearance, having recently been cleaned. The name of Ruston is recorded alongside his wife and daughter, but, as with Clayton, neither his occupation – head of a major engineering firm – nor his service as mayor are recorded. Gary Rook's chapter examines the steps taken to refurbish this grave.

The head of a third city engineering company, William Foster (M.1863, d.1876), is also buried in Eastgate Cemetery. In contrast to his former rivals in business, his memorial is a low rectangular slab of polished pink granite with hipped top. The inscription is brief

Memorial to Nathaniel Clayton (1811–1890), Canwick Road Cemetery. (*Ken Redmore*).

and lacks clarity, though the monument's robust material and solid construction resist corrosion and ensure longevity.

A few of the larger and more ostentatious memorials in the Canwick Road Cemetery are in the form of obelisks. One such, with a height of 3.0m, marks the grave of George Glasier (M.1868), chemical fertiliser manufacturer, who died at the age of 92 in 1900. Another impressive type is the tall pedestal, usually about the size and shape of a pillar box but rectangular in cross section. The adjacent graves of William Battle Maltby (M.1874, d.1877) and his relative John Battle (M.1867, d.1890), chemists and druggists, are both marked in this way. The memorial to Charles Doughty (M.1862, d.1882, seed merchant) is also of this type; it has the additional embellishment of an urn on the top, making the whole monument about 3.2m in height.

Two other memorials in this study are worthy of special note. One is for William Beard (M.1875, draper) who died 1894; it is a striking headstone fashioned in dark grey granite in the Arts and Crafts style of the period. The inscription is carried on a curvaceous scroll draped over the head of the memorial and is flanked by bold leaf shapes and diagonally mounted shields. The other is the restrained but equally impressive white marble memorial to William Watkins (M.1888, d.1926, architect), in Eastgate Cemetery. The lengthy inscription, superbly cut in Roman script, is presented on a small, framed stone with curved top and rectangular shoulders at the head of the grave. One of the uprights is decorated by the masonic symbol of square and compasses.

Most of the remaining memorials included in this study are either crosses – plain Latin or ringed – mounted on stepped bases, or plain headstones with rounded or Gothic pointed tops. The grave of William Ashley (M.1866, d.1888, wine merchant), exceptionally, is a chest tomb. One of the simple headstones, marking the grave of Peter Platts Dickinson (M.1876, d.1918, auctioneer), is unusually small – only 50cm high – though it is enhanced by the short, raised posts topped with small horizontal crosses which stand at each corner of the kerb surrounding the grave.

As far as materials are concerned, the majority of gravestones are made of granite or sandstone. Only one is clearly marked with the name of a Lincoln monumental mason

(Tuttell); the poor condition of some graves makes it impossible to discover inscribed masons' names, especially on kerbs, where they are commonly located. Apart from the examples already noted, there are few examples of interesting, good quality decorative features. One exception is the sculpted angel shown in relief on a flat cross above the grave of Bernard Cannon (M.1880, d.1893, leather and glue manufacturer). For the most part there are no discernible changes in style over the period covered by this sample (1876 to 1930); monumental masons and the families of the deceased were generally very conservative in their choice of gravestone.

Memorial to William Beard (1821–1894), Canwick Road Cemetery. (*Ken Redmore*).

Those who served as city councillors and were subsequently elected mayor were, to varying degrees, men of substance. Their status in the community was conferred as much by their occupations as by their roles in the government of the city. Typically, they were also leading players in one or other of the Lincoln churches or chapels and held prominent roles in a range of local charities and other organisations. Their funerals were invariably big occasions for the city, with relatives, friends and associates filling a large procession of carriages from church to cemetery. It is reported that a scarcely believable crowd of 10,000 people was in the cemetery for the burial of T. J. N. Brogden (M.1854 & 1879) in 1880. (Ironically, Brogden's grave is the only one in the study that cannot be examined; it is now totally enveloped by a large dense bush.)

Yet, despite the prominence of the mayor in Lincoln society, and the splendour of their funerals, the conclusion drawn from this brief survey is that the gravestones of late-nineteenth-century mayors have no consistent level of size, design or quality. None carry the Lincoln arms of cross and fleur-de-lis, and, perhaps surprisingly, only five of the 21 gravestone inscriptions mention the individual's service as mayor. (Rather more – about half – note service as alderman and justice of the peace.) One reason for this omission may be the long interval between an individual's term as mayor (for a single year) and his death. For this sample the average time gap was well over 20 years; only for T. J. N. Brogden, serving his second term as mayor in 1879, was it less than a year. It would appear therefore that the size, quality and design of the memorials of these men reflected the individual's material success and the prominence of his occupation rather than his former status as the leading citizen of Lincoln.

Two Lincoln Monumental Mason Firms: The Businesses of Arthur Howson and Arthur John Long Tuttell

Georgina Collingwood

This chapter explores the families of two businesses much associated with the manufacture of funerary monuments in Lincoln in the nineteenth and twentieth centuries. The extent of family engagement in both businesses is outlined, and the way in which the two firms come together in the early twentieth century is also examined. It should be noted that, by this time period, there were a number of monumental masons active in Lincoln, including William Goodall, whose works moved to Canwick Road in 1874, conveniently close to the cemetery. During the first decade of the twentieth century, others providing the services of monumental masons included the following: William Footit, who advertised extensively in the local press, first from the Great Northern Station Yard and then Portland Street; Jesse Boulton, who had a monumental mason's business in the High Street from at least 1901 until the early 1930s; and Frederick and William Colley, both Saxilby-born stone masons, who had set up a business on Brayford Street by 1874 and had moved to St Mark's, High Street, by 1883, where they were specialising in monumental work. Both of the Colley brothers pursued public office, with William, who was also a Wesleyan preacher, appointed to the Board of Guardians, and Frederick briefly serving as a city councillor and, for a more sustained period, a member of the Lincoln Burial Board. Frederick's sons, Frederick G., William H. and Edward later trained in the business, which continued to operate from St Mark's after the deaths of William and Frederick, in respectively 1895 and 1899, until 1902, after which William H. set up as a monumental mason by himself at nearby premises.

The Howsons

Arthur Howson was born in Lincoln in 1860; his father Eliezer set up the Howson building company in the city around 1859 when he took over the business of John Foster, a successful brick-maker and builder. The Howson family originally lived and worked in Newland and St Mark's Lane, first appearing in Tentercroft Street in the 1871 census when Eliezer and his family moved to number 8. By the 1881 census, Arthur and his two brothers George and Walter were all described as bricklayers or apprentice bricklayers. Arthur's older brother Seth William had already left home by this time, had qualified as a bricklayer and was married with three young children. Seth settled in Eastgate where he was variously described as a bricklayer, house builder, and latterly, upon his death in 1912, as 'monumental mason and builder'.

Headstone made by Seth Howson in Eastgate Cemetery from 1906. (*Georgina Collingwood*).

It could perhaps be assumed that in 1881, Arthur was now employed by his father. On a succession of census returns, Arthur was listed as a bricklayer. He lived on Chelmsford Street (just off Cross Street) and then later moved to 10 Pond Street (now known as St Faith's Street). In 1899 he placed a small notice in the *Lincolnshire Chronicle* to announce he was moving his business premises from Pond Street to Tentercroft Street where his mother was still living. Arthur's first wife, Sekunda, who was German, passed away in 1906, and he married a younger woman, Mabel Simpson in 1908 with whom he had two more children. In 1911 three of his sons were employed as bricklayers (presumably by him or his father as they still lived at home) so it can be fairly confidently stated that the business of building was thriving for 50-year-old Arthur Howson. He was now back living at number 8 Tentercroft Street, where his father, Eliezer, also lived until his death in 1884. Arthur's mother remained there until she died in 1905, when the house must have passed to Arthur, the youngest son.

An article in the *Lincolnshire Echo* in 1931 tells of the business being 'set back' during the First World War because four sons were serving in the British armed forces. In 1921 60 year-old Arthur continued to live at 8 Tentercroft Street, with his 45-year-old wife and

family. He described himself as 'builder, repairer of houses and cottages', along with his son, Fritz, who was then aged 30 and Hermann, aged 28. Harold Felix, 25, was described as 'stone mason assisting father'; the two younger girls Phyllis and Amelia were at home, along with older brother Alfred, a marine engineer, who was visiting with his wife and daughter. The business continued mainly to carry out building work with some monumental work as well. Then, around 1930, a link was forged with the business of Arthur John Long Tuttell.

Arthur John Long Tuttell

Arthur John Long Tuttell was born in Lambeth, London in 1870, and by the 1881 census the family was living in Tewkesbury, Gloucestershire. Arthur's father, George, was a wood and stone carver. Arthur moved to Selby, where he was initially described as a sculptor while living as a boarder in the family of a railway engine driver. His father seemed to have relocated to Grantham where his parents lived until his father's death in 1891. By 1893, in Grantham, his widowed mother, Mary, with Arthur, traded as M. Tuttell and Son, stonemasons. The business was moved to Lincoln in September 1894, as noted in a newspaper report of a dispute with the firm's apprentice, who seemed disinclined to leave Grantham. Arthur married Annie Clarke in Lincoln in 1896. At that time, M. Tuttell and Son, seemed to specialise in ecclesiastical work. In 1899, they were given the important commission of carving a chair for St Mary Magdalene's church in Bailgate, from a design by Mr H. G. Gamble, a well-known and successful Lincoln architect.

In the 1901 census Arthur was listed at 80 Monks Road, Lincoln, with his wife, Sarah Annie, and his niece, Hettie Richardson, as well as a domestic servant. Ten years later, Arthur

A. Tuttell headstone in Eastgate Cemetery from 1915. (*Georgina Collingwood*).

was advertising his services as a monumental mason, with his premises on Corporation Street, in a building with a frontage still used as a shop today. The advertisement mentions 'Headstones or kerbings lettered and fixed complete from 50s. each'. He continued to trade as M. Tuttell and Son following the death of his mother, Mary, in 1910.

By 1911, following the sudden death of his wife in 1904, Arthur was living at 4 Granville Terrace, Bracebridge, with Gertrude Verrinder, a relative and Iris Rita and Iris Kathleen Verrinder, both aged ten, and four-year-old Valmai Thompson. Advertisements placed in two different local newspapers in 1912 in order to find a new tenant for a 'lock up shop in Corporation Street Lincoln' suggested that Arthur owned other properties in Lincoln. There were as well as 'two bay window offices, staircase from street, Corporation Street' in 1926. Another advertisement in the *Lincolnshire Echo* in 1913 promoted 'Memorials fixed everywhere, over 50 in stock. Headstones and kerbing lettered and fixed complete for 50/- Artistic work at no extra cost'.

Arthur had established himself securely in Lincoln by the early years of the twentieth century as a sculptor in stone and wood, and with a reputation for supplying headstones. Many fine examples of his work can be seen in Lincoln's cemeteries as well as in surrounding village churchyards.

During and after the First World War, Arthur Tuttell became an active promotor of the idea of erecting suitable memorials to honour those who had been lost by villages or towns in his local area. One such memorial was erected in the small village of Dalderby, near Horncastle, as reported in the *Lincolnshire Echo* on 5 October 1916:

M. Tuttell & Son premises on Corporation Street, c. 1911. (*Courtesy of Stephen Howson*).

They are in consultation for the erections of several, similar crosses in various parts of Lincolnshire, many parishes feeling the necessity of erecting some memorial to the memory of their men who have died for King and country and their families homestead, and whose bodies rest in graves on foreign soil. It should also be mentioned that to Mr Tuttell is due the inception of the idea.

Some of the war memorial work in Lincoln produced by Arthur Tuttell and his firm is examined elsewhere in this volume in the chapters by Arthur Ward and Andrew Walker.

By 1926, Arthur John Long Tuttell must have moved to 4 Beaumont Terrace, Lincoln, where he passed away in October 1929 aged 60 years. The *Nottingham Journal* reported on 28 October that 'The death took place at Lincoln on Saturday of Mr Arthur John Tuttell, a prominent citizen, who for many years had carried on business as a sculptor. In his younger days he played a prominent part in numerous operatic productions by the Lincoln Amateur Operatic Society'.

He was buried on 30 October at St Swithin's Cemetery. It was at this point that the family became linked with the Howson family of Tentercroft Street.

Bringing together the Tuttell and Howson Names
At the north-west end of Tentercroft Street, near its junction with the High Street, there is a building notable for its green double doors. Next to these are two stone signs, carved

with the names of 'M. Tuttell and Son stonemasons', and 'Arthur Howson and Sons Ltd'. To the side of the adjoining building, high up on the wall, is the large brick sign advertising 'Howson Builders'. The reason for the two different names is that the Howson family took over the business after the death of Arthur Tuttell, keeping the name for the monumental aspects of the business, undoubtedly because of the reputation he had within the city of Lincoln.

The Howson family registered 'Arthur Howson and Sons, Sculptors, Monumental Masons, Builders and Contractors' as a limited company in July 1930 with £3000 in £1 shares. It was reported in 1931 that the 'firm have opened the monumental department more recently under the direction of Mr F. H. Howson, who had many years' practical experience with the late Mr A. J. Tuttell. It has since made rapid strides and a new showroom has been built in

Premises of Arthur Howson & Sons Ltd and M. Tuttell & Son Ltd, at 8 and 6 Tentercroft Street respectively. (*Georgina Collingwood*).

Howson and Tuttell business nameplates on Tentercroft Street premises. (*Andrew Walker*).

Newport in order to enable the firm to cope with the increasing demands from the uphill district'.

Another document shows the Howson company writing to a prospective customer in 1930, suggesting the design for a proposed memorial. Advertisements placed in the *Lincolnshire Echo* declare them to have the 'largest selection in the city, Tentercroft Street and Newport' in 1932 and 1934. However, by 1937, Howson company advertising does not mention monuments at all, only building work, reflecting that the two parts of the business were being run independently of each other. By 1939, Arthur described himself as a 'retired builder', Hermann as a 'building works manager', Alfred as a 'master builder' and Fritz was a 'builder'. It was only Felix Harold who was listed in the 1939 Register as a 'monumental mason (master)'. Arthur Howson died later in 1939, and was buried in Canwick Road cemetery, followed in 1940 by his son Fritz and, later in the same year, youngest son, Felix Harold. Alfred died in 1952 and Hermann in 1953.

As the sign on the Tentercroft Road building indicates, M. Tuttell and Son continues to operate as stonemasons. Examples of all of these monumental masons' work can be seen in the city's cemeteries.

LINCOLN CREMATORIUM
Andrew Walker

Following a Lincoln woman's death notice appearing in the *Daily Telegraph*, in which details of her funeral and cremation in Grimsby were included, Charles Brook of 'London SE9' wrote to the *Lincolnshire Echo* in January 1963 declaring that 'If there is still no crematorium at Lincoln, as a former citizen, I am shocked.' According to figures from the Office for National Statistics, in 1963 in Great Britain some 41% of those who died were now cremated, in 177 crematoria situated across the country. The earliest modern crematorium had been opened in 1885 in Woking, Surrey, and, following the Cremation Acts of 1900 and 1902 which allowed public provision for individuals who wished to be cremated, the first municipal crematorium was opened in Hull in 1904.

The lack of a crematorium in Lincoln had been the cause of some comment nearly twenty years before Charles Brook's letter. In October 1943, a provisional crematorium plan was approved by Lincoln City Council, which included alternative schemes for a crematorium to be attached to an existing cemetery and one on a site entirely on its own. By 1947, demand for a crematorium in the city had been acknowledged and land provisionally reserved for this purpose had been secured on the Boultham Moor estate. As the *Lincolnshire Echo* noted on 1 July 1949, if a cremation were requested, it had to take place at one of the neighbouring cities of Nottingham, Leicester and Hull. In the same report, the Assistant Registrar of Cemeteries in Lincoln, G.W. Teer, estimated that about 10 per cent of people who die in Lincoln would be cremated if a crematorium were available in the city. Mr Teer's forecast perhaps underestimated the possible demand. In 1949, in Great Britain some 14 per cent of those who died that year were cremated, and it was acknowledged that in areas where crematoria were situated, the percentage of cremations was significantly higher. However, as was reported at a conference in Boston on 24 April 1950 to discuss whether a crematorium should be built in south Lincolnshire, rural people were less inclined to opt for cremation than townspeople.

The view of the city's Parks, Markets and Cemeteries Committee in September 1957 was that the time was still not right for a crematorium, citing the limited availability of suitable land and the costs associated with the building and maintenance of such a facility. On 29 July 1960, the *Lincolnshire Echo* reported that an average of between 100 and 150 Lincoln people were cremated each year, the majority of them at either Nottingham's crematorium at Wilford Hill Cemetery, opened in 1931, or Grimsby's which had been operational since 1954. A certain impatience at the lack of progress on this matter was evident in The Gossiper's column in the *Lincolnshire Echo* on 5 January 1965 when, under the heading 'Lincoln lags behind', it was reported that Chatham in Kent, with a population of 50,000, and a rateable value of £1.75m had a crematorium, opened in 1959, whilst Lincoln, with a population of 80,000 and a rateable value of £2.5m does not. (This comparison was a little unfair since the crematorium at Chatham also served the needs of the neighbouring populous Medway towns.) Across Great Britain, 44 per cent of those who died in 1965 were cremated. The following year saw the opening of two other Lincolnshire crematoria at Boston and Grantham; Scunthorpe's Woodlands Crematorium had been opened in 1964. The absence of one in the county town looked increasingly conspicuous.

Finally, in 1967, work began on the construction of a crematorium on Washingborough Road, next to existing cemeteries, on a ten-acre, landscaped site, with 20 transplanted mature trees. The building itself was set back from the road and parking for 30 cars was included in the plans. The facilities comprised a chapel, with a shallow domed roof, which accommodated 60 to 70 mourners and provision for more if needed in a side aisle; a smaller structure adjoining the main building for the display of a book of remembrance; a chauffeurs' waiting room; and a gas-fired twin furnace from which would emanate no visible smoke. The structure was designed as a simple, dignified building by the City Architect, Mr R.R. Alexander, and his staff, with David Vale as the project architect. Its main walls were built of hand-made bricks and the material used for the chimney was reconstructed stone. Much press interest was also paid to the chapel's innovative stereophonic sound system.

By its official opening in November 1968, the building had cost £93,000 to construct. The opening ceremony was a notable one, not least because of the late arrival of the civic party

The crematorium under construction, 1968. (*Courtesy of Lincoln Central Library, Lincolnshire County Council/GLL. Ref. LCL7932*).

owing to a misunderstanding over the start time. The Bishop of Lincoln, the Rt Rev. Kenneth Riches, who had also officiated at the openings of the crematoria at Scunthorpe, Boston and Grantham, had begun the service before the mayor, Councillor Ralph Wadsworth, and his entourage had arrived. Once the late mayor and other members of the civic party had taken their places, the bishop declared that they had better start again. In his speech declaring the building open, the mayor commented that the building had not come into being without a great deal of heart searching and argument. The mayor was referring in part to lively debates within the council regarding whether or not to employ an open or selective tendering process to source suppliers for the crematorium project. In the end, a selective tendering process was used which limited the number of suppliers who could compete for work on the initiative. Another problem relating to the construction of the crematorium was a two-year delay on commencement of the project which was caused by what was referred to at the time as the 'national economic situation', linked to a trade depression and the devaluation of sterling.

The interest in the new crematorium was so great that a series of open days were planned over the first twelve months of its operation. As the *Lincolnshire Echo* reported on 2 December 1968, the first of these had taken place on the previous Sunday when over 750 people had attended. The purpose of such events, the newspaper noted, was 'to let people see what goes on in a crematorium and to get rid of the idea that it is some big mystery.' The year in which

The original crematorium building. (*Andrew Walker*).

Lincoln's crematorium opened was the first year in Great Britain when cremations exceeded burials, with 51 per cent of the dead being cremated.

More recent figures reveal the considerable increase in the proportion of cremations since the 1960s, with 78 per cent of Great Britain's dead being cremated in 2021. The increased demand has led to recent significant development and refurbishment work at the Lincoln crematorium. This began in April 2021 and involved an upgrade to the main crematorium building, including the crematory and committal areas, and the installation of two new cremators. As part of the works, a second chapel has been added, which opened in July 2021, together with the setting out of additional car parking spaces.

With increasing concerns about the environment, it will be interesting to see whether existing high levels of demand for cremations will continue. The average cremation releases 400 kilograms of carbon dioxide and the fumes created include a number of toxins such as vaporised mercury, from tooth fillings. More environmentally friendly body disposal alternatives including 'green' burials, though land-hungry, and aquamation, a process of alkaline hydrolysis, might perhaps become more prevalent in the future.

The new crematorium building. (*Andrew Walker*).

LONG LEYS CEMETERY

Abigail Hunt

In 2006, City of Lincoln Council set up a working group to evaluate possible options for a new cemetery in Lincoln, as the other cemeteries were approaching their full capacity whilst the demand for burial space in the city continued. It was the Burial Land Working Group which decided that the site on Long Leys Road was the most viable option in the city. The full design and project management of the Long Leys Cemetery Project was led by Dunn and Co. and delivered by Harrison Design Development.

Long Leys is the newest cemetery in Lincoln, situated roughly two kilometres to the north west of city centre on the west-facing slope of the Jurassic ridge that runs north from the city. The site has an elevation of 15 metres to the west and 60 metres to the east, and has a subsoil of middle lias clay and shale. The cemetery is entered from Long Leys Road to the west, is bounded by the A46 to the north, open pasture land to the east, and a modern housing estate to the south, which was formerly the site of St George's Hospital. The cemetery was proposed in the early 2000s and opened in July 2014, at a cost of £1.2 million, with the aim of providing burial space in Lincoln for a period of 30 to 50 years. It has over 4000 plots for burial and also features a flower meadow for green burials, a modern toilet block, and car parking facilities.

Entrance gates at Long Leys Cemetery. (*Andrew Walker*).

City of Lincoln Council signage at the cemetery. (*Andrew Walker*).

The cemetery site appears to have been a location associated with Roman settlement. As Geoff Tann's earlier chapter reveals, Roman interments have been found in close proximity, near to the road bridge under the Lincoln bypass. In 2007, archaeological work on the cemetery site found evidence of Romano British activity, dating from the early to mid-second century AD. This land appeared to continue in use until the fourth century AD, possibly being used as the location of a country residence, such as a farmstead or villa estate, belonging to a wealthy family.

Further archaeological work was conducted on the cemetery site in 2017. The evidence uncovered indicated that there had been buildings in use there throughout most of the fourth century AD, until these were abandoned and then demolished, possibly through burning as represented by the presence of burnt limestone and charcoal. It also suggested that human activity on the site continued after the buildings had been destroyed. By the end of the fourth century, however, the site had been abandoned.

No evidence of activity immediately following the Roman period was found on the site. Over subsequent centuries, the area was covered by sediment that had washed down the

New graves, with object-based tributes. (*Andrew Walker*).

slope on which the cemetery is now located. Further activity was evidenced by surviving ridge and furrow, indicating medieval open field systems and arable farming, which dated to between the thirteenth and fifteenth centuries AD. There is very little evidence for other activity until the modern period. Before its recent redevelopment, the site was home to Park Riding School and Hunting Stables, where horses were grazed and stabled.

The aim of the Long Leys Cemetery Project was to provide a space for burials (including cremations) and the bereaved that was both attractive and peaceful, whilst ensuring the city had burial capacity for another 50 years. The scheme involved designing a drainage system that made the site suitable for burials, which included a feature pond and underground retention tanks, building new office and maintenance buildings, a storage yard, new car parks and roadways, a new footpath to link the cemetery to nearby residential areas, 4700 burial plots, memorial gardens, seated areas, and landscaping. The contractors were also commissioned to provide the City of Lincoln Council with a comprehensive management plan for the cemetery.

One contentious issue during the development of the new cemetery appears to have been the fact that interment costs were higher than in Lincoln's other cemeteries. This issue was covered in the local press, with City of Lincoln Council representatives justifying the

The maturing landscaped gardens, which are a feature of the cemetery. (*Andrew Walker*).

higher costs because of the expense of additional labour required to dig the clay soil here and also to recoup some of the £1.2 million that was spent on creating the new cemetery. Interestingly, nearly a decade later, the costs remain higher than the other cemeteries with an adult grave space in Long Leys Cemetery costing Lincoln residents £715.00 and non-residents £1430,00, compared to £620.00 and £1240.00 in Newport, Canwick, St Swithin's, and Eastgate cemeteries.

The new cemetery opened in 2014, approximately 100 years after the last new cemetery opened in the city, allowing people to buy plots in advance to be interred with their loved ones or to ensure their burial was organised well in advance of their death, which was no longer possible at the other cemeteries. By 2023, the pond had matured and appeared to be a beautiful natural feature rather than a functional drainage pond. Like all the cemeteries in Lincoln the grounds and landscaping are well cared for by the city's council, and there are clusters of modern graves close to the entrance and higher up on the slope to the east.

As with all cemeteries, it is possible to identify burial trends, in this case very recent ones. The headstones tend to be black, polished granite, with personal tributes to the individual buried in the plot, and with some family plots. Since the graves are all recent, there are many floral and object-based tributes by the headstones.

THE LINCOLN GRAVE RESTORATION PROJECT

Gary Rook

The final resting places of two of Lincoln's most influential Victorians can be found at either end of one of the city's most secluded cemeteries. Industrialist Joseph Ruston and architect William Watkins are buried in the rarely visited Eastgate cemetery (originally known as the cemetery of St Peter-in-Eastgate). Indeed, this small, quiet and totally enclosed burial ground is the final resting place of many prominent Lincoln movers and shakers from that period and is well worth a visit. Joseph Ruston's career, philanthropy and major impact upon Lincoln life have been well documented over the years. The name of Ruston still resonates strongly with many local folk.

His funeral in 1897 was reputed to have been the largest ever attended in the county. Strange, then, that his family plot with a decorative Celtic cross has become so neglected over the ensuing period. His immense wealth, large family, numerous business legacies and civic support did not seem to protect his grave from being almost forgotten. It seemed, therefore, a shame that someone who had done so much to put Lincoln on the map had, to all intents and purposes, been forgotten. Consequently, a small group of Lincoln enthusiasts decided to do something positive and attempt to restore the plot to its former glory.

A specialist stonemason was engaged to investigate what could be done especially with regard to the degraded lettering detailing the various members of Joseph's Ruston's family who were also subsequently buried in the plot. Once a renovation plan and budget had been agreed, the next challenge was to try and locate a family member who would be able to sign a council consent form to give the required permission. Two months of detective work, creating a Ruston family tree, finally paid dividends with the discovery of a great-great-great grandson living on the south coast of England who was more than willing to give the go ahead.

The final task was to raise the money. Thanks to some very generous donations from people who wished to preserve aspects of Lincoln heritage the target was reached very quickly and the restoration works commenced. Careful cleaning work by the stonemason worked wonders, as did the eventual sourcing of half a tonne of Cornish blue granite chippings from a Derbyshire quarry to match exactly the rather jaded originals. City of Lincoln Council assisted by removing the overhanging branches that were beginning to impact upon the site. The final result was a transformed monument to a great citizen of Lincoln. On a beautiful sunny July morning in 2022 a small 'opening' ceremony was held and attended by two of Joseph Ruston's descendants.

On the opposite side of Eastgate Cemetery can be found the smaller, but nonetheless still important, grave of the acclaimed architect William Watkins, who died in 1926. Similar

The Ruston grave plot before restoration. (*Gary Rook*).

to Joseph Ruston, Watkins's claim to fame has been well documented, although he is still relatively unknown to the thousands of people who pass by his many buildings each day in Lincoln and elsewhere. Watkins introduced Lincoln to the decorative opportunities of using terracotta tiles and mouldings. His building designs during the late Victorian period have left an indelible mark on the city's landscape. Many consider William Watkins's most memorable buildings to be what was originally called Christ's Hospital School for Girls on Lindum Road, along with the Constitutional Club further down the road. These are two excellent examples of his work but there are many others located all over the city.

Watkins was a man who changed the architectural face of Lincoln, yet his grave was overgrown, unreadable and certainly not becoming of someone who dedicated his life to design and detail. The same group of keen Lincoln history enthusiasts set about raising the funds required to try and return the headstone and kerb stones to something similar to their original state. Again, a family tree had to be created and researched in order to track down descendants, who in turn could provide the necessary permissions. After a few false starts a great-great-great grandson was eventually located in Vancouver and he agreed to any improvement works to the grave of his illustrious forefather.

The Ruston grave plot after restoration. (*Gary Rook*).

The group's members are keen to continue to identify and restore and clean other important graves for future generations to visit and explore. In our sights at the moment are the graves of Sir Richard Ellison and Nathaniel Clayton. Sir Richard Ellison was the last owner of Boultham Hall. The ornate Angel which marks his grave in St Helen's churchyard is blackened by years of soot from nearby factories and is unreadable. The family plot of the Victorian industrialist Nathaniel Clayton in Canwick Road cemetery has suffered damage to the metal plaque and is in need of specialist repair.

However, we feel strongly that we must not overlook contributions made to the city by lesser-known individuals and we will continue to identify other worthy graves in need of restoration and attempt to give them the attention they deserve.

A Few Thoughts on Life, Death and Funerals Over the Last Thirty Years

Jonathan Whiting

When I joined the funeral profession in the late 1980s my impression was that both the profession and society's attitude towards death and funerals had not changed much for many decades before that. Whilst the first stirrings of change were occurring in some cities, here in Lincolnshire every funeral was religious and traditional in every way. Even cremation was considered a bit progressive by some. A funeral arranger would not ask whether the deceased would want a religious or non-religious ceremony but simply what denomination would be appropriate. Most services were still held in church before going on to the cemetery or, for some, the crematorium. The majority of funerals for residents of the more rural villages involved burial in the village churchyard after a service in the church. Nowadays, with a large majority of funerals being cremations, the crematorium chapel is in constant demand. It is sad to see many cemetery chapels have not been kept in use and are falling into disrepair. It is also interesting to note that churchyards and cemeteries now provide areas set aside for cremated remains. A while ago this would be a little corner somewhere; now many are substantial sections of the burial ground.

I do not remember which year it was but I would guess it was around 1990 or 1991 when a lady came to arrange a funeral for her husband and said he had wanted a non-religious

Jonathan Whiting's premises on Queen Street in 2010. (*Jonathan Whiting*).

ceremony. That caused a bit of a panic initially as it was a completely new situation. I ended up leading the ceremony at the crematorium chapel as there were no non-religious celebrants at that time. Non-religious ceremonies became more popular through the 1990s but were still very much in the minority. At the same time people gradually started requesting more personalised funerals. We have moved from a choice, in the 1990s, of three or four types of coffin to a selection from, potentially, hundreds nowadays. We can offer various forms of transport beyond the standard hearse, with several different types of vehicles having been adapted to funeral use. Mourners are often asked not to dress in black, occasionally even to follow a theme. Music is one of the best ways to express emotion. These days, pretty much anything goes; it is a case of what is appropriate for the individual rather than what everyone else expects. There have been funerals where mourners have been invited to dance in the aisle. Only a few years ago, that would have been completely unthinkable.

Today's range of choices is a big improvement. It is far easier to arrange a fitting goodbye for anyone and that must be a good thing.

A funeral ready to go in 2003: Jonathan Whiting in the foreground flanked by his son, Edward and father-in-law, Colin. (*Jonathan Whiting*).

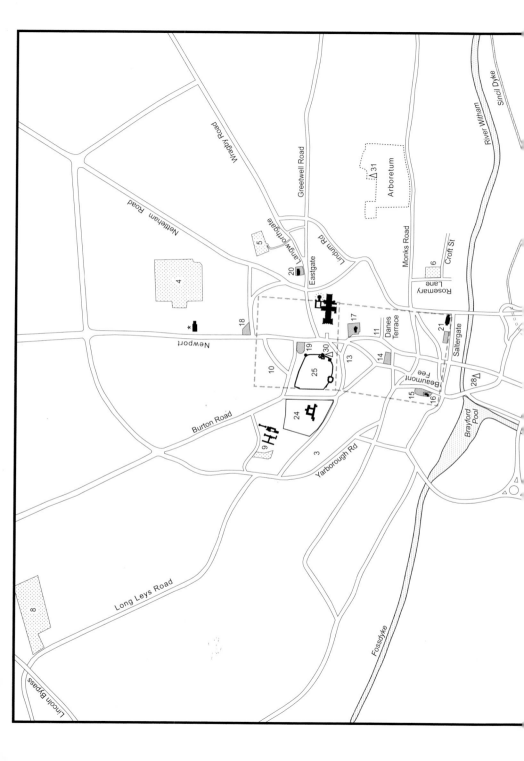

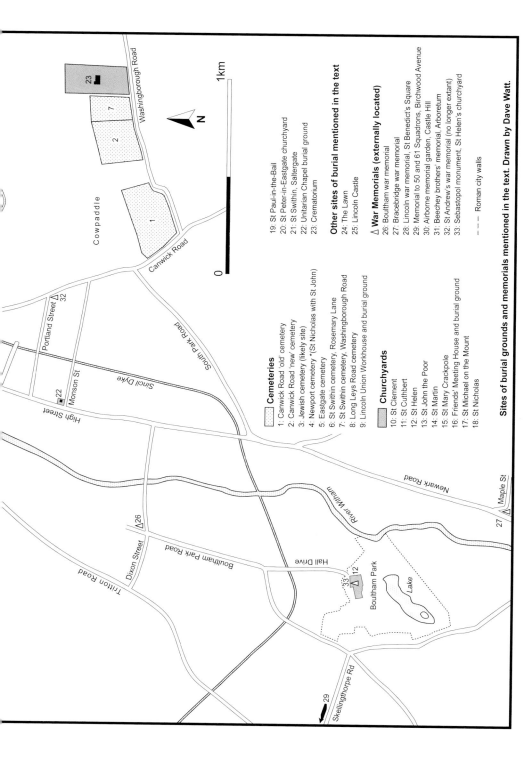

Cemeteries
1: Canwick Road 'old' cemetery
2: Canwick Road 'new' cemetery
3: Jewish cemetery (likely site)
4: Newport cemetery *(St Nicholas with St John)
5: Eastgate cemetery
6: St Swithin cemetery, Rosemary Lane
7: St Swithin cemetery, Washingborough Road
8: Long Leys Road cemetery
9: Lincoln Union Workhouse and burial ground

Churchyards
10: St Clement
11: St Cuthbert
12: St Helen
13: St John the Poor
14: St Martin
15: St Mary Crackpole
16: Friends' Meeting House and burial ground
17: St Michael on the Mount
18: St Nicholas

19: St Paul-in-the-Bail
20: St Peter-in-Eastgate churchyard
21: St Swithin, Saltergate
22: Unitarian Chapel burial ground
23: Crematorium

Other sites of burial mentioned in the text
24: The Lawn
25: Lincoln Castle

△ **War Memorials (externally located)**
26: Boultham war memorial
27: Bracebridge war memorial
28: Lincoln war memorial, St Benedict's Square
29: Memorial to 50 and 61 Squadrons, Birchwood Avenue
30: Airborne memorial garden, Castle Hill
31: Beechey brothers' memorial, Arboretum
32: St Andrew's war memorial (no longer extant)
33: Sebastopol monument, St Helen's churchyard

– – – – Roman city walls

Sites of burial grounds and memorials mentioned in the text. Drawn by Dave Watt.

Suggestions for further reading:

PRIMARY SOURCES:
Lincolnshire Chronicle. Lincolnshire Echo. Stamford Mercury. Kelly's *Directories of Lincolnshire.* Ruddock's *Lincoln City Directories.* White's *Directories of Lincolnshire.*

SECONDARY SOURCES:
Allen, M. R., Oakley, E. and Trott, K., *Archaeological Scheme of Works Report: Lincoln College, Lincoln, Lincolnshire, Volume 1: Report and Figures,* Allen Archaeology Ltd, Lincoln, 2012. https://doi.org/10.5284/1024246.

Brace, Harold, (ed.) *The First Minute Book of the Gainsborough Monthly Meeting of the Society of Friends 1669–1719,* vols 1–3, Lincoln Record Society, 1948–51.

Butler, David, *The Quaker Meeting Houses of Britain,* Friends Historical Society, London, 1989.

Casswell, C., *Archaeological excavation report: archaeological excavation at the Sarah Swift Building, Brayford Wharf East, Lincoln,* Allen Archaeology Limited, Lincoln, 2017. https://doi.org/10.5284/1100375.

Commonwealth War Graves Commission, *Lincoln (Eastgate) (or St. Peter's) Cemetery, Cemetery Details.* https://www.cwgc.org/visit-us/find-cemeteries-memorials/cemetery-details/41577/lincoln-eastgate-or-st-peter-s-cemetery/, 2023.

Credland, Michael, *The First World War Memorials of Lincolnshire*, Society for Lincolnshire History and Archaeology, Lincoln, 2014.

Davies, Susan, *Quakerism in Lincolnshire,* Yard Publishing Services, Lincoln, 1989.

Draper, Anna, 'The hidden secrets of Lincoln's forgotten Victorian cemetery', Lincolnshire Live. https://www.lincolnshirelive.co.uk/news/local-news/hidden-secrets-forgotten-victorian-cemetery-1860135, 3 August, 2018.

Hill, Francis, *Medieval Lincoln*, Cambridge University Press, Cambridge, 1948.

Hill, Francis, *Victorian Lincoln*, Cambridge University Press, Cambridge, 1974.

Jones, Michael J., *Lincoln: History and Guide. Third Edition*, History Press, Cheltenham, 2011.

Jones, Michael J., *Roman Lincoln: Conquest, Colony and Capital,* The History Press, Stroud, (Revised edition), 2011.

Jones, Michael J.; Stocker, David; and Vince, Alan, *The City by the Pool*, (Stocker, David, ed.), Oxbow Books, Oxford, 2003.

Mills, Dennis and Wheeler, Robert C., eds, *Historic Town Plans of Lincoln, 1610–1920,* published for the Lincoln Record Society and the Survey of Lincoln by Boydell and Brewer, Woodbridge, 2004.

Overton, J. H., and Wordsworth, Elizabeth, *Life of Christopher Wordsworth*, Rivingtons, London, 1888.

Page, A.B., ed., 'Archaeology in Lincolnshire and South Humberside, 1984' in *Lincolnshire History and Archaeology,* 20 (1985), pp. 71–2.

Pevsner, Nikolaus and Harris, John, *The Buildings of England: Lincolnshire. Second Edition,* (Antram, Nicholas, ed.) Penguin Books, Harmondsworth, 1989.

Rayner, T., *Archaeological Scheme of Works Report: Land Off Newport, Lincoln,* Allen Archaeology Ltd, Lincoln, 2016. Https://Doi.Org/10.5284/1100345.

Snell, Keith, *Parish and Belonging. Community, Identity and Welfare in England and Wales, 1700–1950,* Cambridge University Press, Cambridge, 2006.

Stocker, David, 'The Archaeology of the Reformation in Lincoln', *Lincolnshire History and Archaeology,* 25 (1990), pp. 18–32.

Stocker, David, 'Aristocrats, burghers and their markets: patterns in the foundation of Lincoln's urban churches', in Hadley, Dawn and ten Harkel, Letty, eds, *Everyday Life in Viking-Age Towns: Social Approaches to Towns in England and Ireland, c. 800–1100,* Oxbow Books, Oxford, 2013, pp. 119–43.

Sympson, T., *A Short Account of the Old and of the New Lincoln County Hospitals,* James Williamson, Lincoln, 1878.

Related chapters in The Survey of Lincoln's Neighbourhood book series:

In *Wigford: Historic Lincoln South of the River* (2000):
Jones, Michael J., 'Origins to end of Roman period'. pp. 2–3.
Vince, Alan, 'Anglo-Saxon Wigford', pp. 4–5.

In *Monks Road: Lincoln's East End Through Time* (2006):
Dixon, Ron, 'The discovery of a medieval cemetery', pp. 11–12.

In *Lincoln's West End: A History,* (2008):
Johnson, Chris, 'Between "Paradise" and a rubbish dump', pp. 8–10.
Jones, Michael J., 'The West End's early history and archaeology', p. 4.

In *Uphill Lincoln I: Burton Road, Newport and the Ermine Estate* (2009):
Jones, Michael J., 'Roman occupation west and north of the Upper Enclosure', pp. 4–5.
Johnson, Chris, 'Cemeteries and churchyards', pp. 48–50.
Stocker, David, 'The medieval suburbs of Newport and Westcastle', pp. 7–10.

In *Uphill Lincoln II: The North-Eastern Suburbs* (2010):
Jones, Michael J., 'Archaeology and prehistory in the neighbourhood', pp. 4–5.

In *South-East Lincoln: Canwick Road, South Common, St Catherine's and Bracebridge* (2011):
Broughton, Derek, 'The Canwick Road cemeteries and crematorium', pp. 74–77.
Jones, Michael J., 'Archaeology of the south-eastern suburbs', pp. 5–8.
Yeates-Langley, Ann, 'The Malandry', pp. 11–13.

In *Boultham and Swallowbeck: Lincoln's South-Western Suburbs* (2013):
Ward, Arthur, 'Churches, chapels and mission rooms', pp. 57–60.

In *Lincoln's City Centre: South of the River Witham* (2016):
MacIntosh, Alastair, 'Recent archaeological investigations in Wigford', pp. 6–9.
Ward, Arthur, 'Anglican churches', pp. 16–20.

Websites:
https://arcade.lincoln.gov.uk
http://www.britishnewspaperarchive.co.uk
www.calmview.eu/lincolnshirearchives/calmview/
www.cremation.org.uk/progress-of-cremation-united-kingdom
www.debs.ac.uk (Discovering England's burial spaces)
www.lincoln.gov.uk/visitors/archaeology-heritage-1/5
www.lincoln-record-society.org.uk
www.lincolnshire.gov.uk/historic-environment/historic-environment-record
www.slha.org.uk

To discover details of individual graves in Lincoln cemeteries, please see:
www.lincoln.gov.uk/l/find-grave-burial-site-lincoln